D1529029

Shadows in the Jungle

MACV-SOG's Secret War in Vietnam
Charles J. McArthur

Castle Vale Publishers Ltd

© **Copyright 2025 – All rights reserved.**

The content contained within this book may not be reproduced, duplicated or transmitted without direct written permission from the author or the publisher.

Under no circumstances will any blame or legal responsibility be held against the publisher, or author, for any damages, reparation, or monetary loss due to the information contained within this book, either directly or indirectly.

Legal Notice: This book is copyright protected. It is only for personal use. You cannot amend, distribute, sell, use, quote or paraphrase any part, or the content within this book, without the consent of the author or publisher.

Disclaimer Notice: Please note the information contained within this document is for educational and entertainment purposes only. All effort has been executed to present accurate, up to date, reliable, complete information. No warranties of any kind are declared or implied. The content within this book has been derived from various sources. By reading this document, the reader agrees that under no circumstances is the author responsible for any losses, direct or indirect, that are incurred as a result of the use of the information contained within this document, including, but not limited to, errors, omissions, or inaccuracies.

Cover photo: Members of U.S. Navy SEAL Team One on the Bassac River, south of Saigon, aboard a SEAL Team Assault Boat, November 1967. (National Archives)

Contents

Introduction

Stepping into the Shadows of Vietnam

Welcome to this in-depth exploration of the **Military Assistance Command, Vietnam – Studies and Observations Group (MACV-SOG)**—an elite unit whose clandestine missions during the Vietnam War pushed the boundaries of modern warfare. Since its inception in 1964, MACV-SOG operated under a shroud of secrecy, executing covert operations in some of the most unforgiving environments on Earth. In this opening chapter, we will set the stage for understanding the origins, nature, and lasting importance of this extraordinary group. We will begin by contextualizing the broader conflict in Vietnam, examine the political and strategic climates that birthed SOG, and preview the journey ahead. Throughout, we will maintain a sense of empathy for the many perspectives involved, recognizing the complexity of a war that shaped not only the soldiers who fought it but also the civilians caught in its wake.[1]

Figure 1 – MACV-SOG
Unofficial Patch

The War That Refused to Stay in the Shadows

The Vietnam War in Brief

Long before the United States escalated its involvement, Vietnam had already endured decades of conflict and colonial domination. Following World War II, the French attempted to reclaim their former colony in Indochina, only to be met with determined resistance from the Viet Minh under Ho Chi Minh's leadership.[2] By 1954, the French were decisively defeated at Dien Bien Phu, setting the stage for the Geneva Accords, which temporarily divided Vietnam at the 17th Parallel. North Vietnam, under Ho Chi Minh, championed communism, while South Vietnam, supported by Western nations, pursued a non-communist path under leaders such as Ngo Dinh Diem.[3]

Throughout the 1950s and early 1960s, the United States steadily increased its advisory and financial support to South Vietnam.[4]

Fears of the so-called "domino theory"—the notion that if one nation in Southeast Asia fell to communism, others would follow—drove American involvement.[5] Under Presidents Eisenhower, Kennedy, and later Johnson, the U.S. presence evolved from a handful of military advisers to tens of thousands of troops on the ground. By the mid-1960s, direct combat operations had become an inescapable reality.

Yet the war in Vietnam proved elusive. While U.S. forces possessed formidable firepower and air superiority, the Viet Cong (VC) and North Vietnamese Army (NVA) excelled at guerrilla tactics, leveraging dense jungles and hidden trails for concealment.[6] For many American military leaders, conventional tactics that had once succeeded in Europe or Korea now seemed insufficient. A new kind of warfare, blending covert operations with psychological and unconventional tactics, came to be viewed as essential. Out of this need emerged MACV-SOG: a small, secretive group tasked with stepping beyond official boundaries—both literally and figuratively—to wage a hidden war.

The Seeds of a Covert Campaign

Officially formed as the "Studies and Observations Group," MACV-SOG was placed under the umbrella of the Military Assistance Command, Vietnam (MACV). The innocuous-sounding name belied its high-risk missions, many of which took place in neighboring countries like Laos and Cambodia—regions where the U.S. was not formally permitted to wage war.[7] As a result, SOG operators often found themselves in a moral and diplomatic minefield, conducting missions their own government could not publicly acknowledge.[8]

Secrecy was not merely a strategic choice; it was also a survival mechanism. SOG operators relied on speed, stealth, and the element of surprise, carrying out reconnaissance, sabotage, and rescue missions in areas where the enemy reigned supreme. This need for concealment shaped every aspect of their

CHARLES J. MCARTHUR

service—from training to equipment, from mission briefings to the very language used in official reports.

Why Focus on MACV-SOG?

A Uniquely High-Risk Undertaking

Special operations have always attracted a certain mystique, with stories of daring raids and behind-the-lines heroics capturing the popular imagination. But MACV-SOG stood apart for the sheer scale of danger in which its men found themselves. Operating in small teams, often outnumbered by enemy forces, SOG recon units had some of the highest casualty rates in U.S. military history—yet they persisted because their missions were deemed vital.[9]

Historical records, once sealed and now partially declassified, show SOG teams infiltrating as far as 30 miles behind enemy lines with little to no backup.[10] One ex-SOG member, Sergeant Alvin "Buck" Daniels, recounted in a 1985 interview how "we'd sometimes step foot in places we knew we were never supposed to be. If we got pinned down, there were moments we thought no one was ever coming for us. But we did it because we had a job that could save lives elsewhere."[11] These testimonies illustrate why SOG's story is not merely another war tale but a testament to the extremes of covert warfare.

Under the Shadow of Official Denial

During the height of the conflict, many of SOG's operations were categorically denied by U.S. officials.[12] Leaders in Washington feared that acknowledging cross-border missions in Laos and Cambodia could provoke international backlash or even draw other powers more directly into the war. Hence, SOG operators went about their tasks with the understanding that their government might disavow them if their presence was discovered. This was despite the fact northern enemy forces were using both Laos and Cambodia for their logistical supply routes into South Vietnam.

For the men in the field, this led to a constant tension between duty and anonymity. Staff Sergeant James Elkins, interviewed for an oral history project decades later, reflected, "You knew the mission was essential, but if something happened, your family might never know the truth. There wouldn't be a headline saying 'SOG Team Lost in Laos' because officially we weren't there. It took a certain mindset to accept that."[13] This aspect of SOG's legacy underscores the personal sacrifices of those who fought in silence.

Setting the Stage for a New Kind of Warfare

The Emergence of Unconventional Tactics

By the early 1960s, American commanders recognized that conventional military strategies were yielding mixed results in Vietnam's dense jungles and hidden supply routes.[14] Search-and-destroy missions clashed with guerrilla ambushes; sweeping ground operations failed to uproot a mobile, entrenched enemy. The political climate discouraged overt expansion of the war into Laos and Cambodia, though the North Vietnamese heavily used those territories for transporting men and materiel.

In this environment, Special Forces units—particularly the Green Berets—began experimenting with more flexible, covert methods. They trained local militias, gathered real-time intelligence on enemy movements, and carried out small-scale raids meant to disorient the VC and NVA. Building on these efforts, MACV-SOG was officially established in January 1964, drawing from the most seasoned operators in the Special Forces (Green Berets), the Navy's Underwater Demolition Teams (SEALS), and other specialized outfits such as Marine Recon and Air Force units.[15]

Secrecy as a Strategic Asset

The emphasis on secrecy went beyond just a desire for strategic advantage. Because SOG was crossing international boundaries, plausible deniability became essential at the highest levels of government.[16] Many missions were labeled with code names like "Shining Brass" or "Prairie Fire" to mask their real objectives. Even routine after-action reports were highly classified, ensuring that details rarely made their way into the mainstream reporting of the war.

For SOG operators, this secrecy was both an asset and a burden. It granted them freedom to act outside the usual bureaucratic constraints, but it also meant that their successes—and failures—would remain largely unacknowledged. Soldiers who survived harrowing engagements could not celebrate or openly discuss their achievements; families of the fallen sometimes went years without the full truth of how their loved ones died.[17]

The Human Cost and Moral Weight

Empathy for All Involved

One cannot discuss SOG without recognizing the war's human dimension. Every mission took place amid the backdrop of villages, towns, and rural communities already reeling from the conflict's devastation. Soldiers—both American and Vietnamese—bore the trauma of constant uncertainty, while civilians often found themselves pawns in a broader strategic struggle.[18]

SOG operators often relied on local allies, such as the Montagnard tribespeople of Vietnam's Central Highlands, who shared their knowledge of the terrain and guided teams along perilous routes. While these alliances proved fruitful, they also placed the Montagnards in direct conflict with the NVA and VC. Many Indigenous fighters faced harsh reprisals after the war. Understanding their experiences demands empathy for populations whose lives were uprooted by the clandestine nature of conflict.

Reconciling Secrecy with Sacrifice

The quiet heroism of MACV-SOG extended beyond the battlefield. Families in the United States were often told little about their relatives' activities. Wives, parents, and children watched in confusion as censored letters or vague official statements arrived. If a soldier went missing, official records offered few details. This secrecy protected missions but also deepened the anguish for loved ones seeking closure.[19]

Over time, some operators struggled with the emotional toll. Interviews years later describe nightmares and enduring guilt, especially when forced to leave behind the remains of comrades or local allies to ensure the rest of the team could escape. One specialist's private journal, discovered after his death, read, "We did what we had to do, but I can still hear the voices in the jungle at night."[20] His reflection captures the haunting personal weight carried by SOG veterans.

A Preview of the Journey Ahead

What This Book Will Cover

In the chapters that follow, we will delve into every facet of MACV-SOG's story. From the historical context that shaped the Vietnam War to the formation of this elite unit, from the remarkable missions they carried out to the lasting impact of their actions, each section builds a comprehensive portrait.[21] We will explore:

1. **Historical Context** – How Vietnam's colonial past and Cold War tensions paved the way for an unconventional war.

2. **Formation of MACV-SOG** – The key players and strategic thinking that brought SOG into being.

3. **Structure and Organization** – The command hierarchies, small-team compositions, and advanced training that defined SOG's operations.

4. **Famous Missions and Special Operations** – Detailed accounts of cross-border raids, reconnaissance operations, and daring extractions like Shining Brass and Prairie Fire.

5. **Equipment, Weaponry, and Tactics** – How specialized gear and tactics gave SOG its covert edge.

6. **Key Personnel and Notable Heroes** – Stories of valor and leadership from both Americans and their Indigenous allies.

7. **Famous Battles and Engagements** – Where SOG operators influenced broader conflicts, such as at Lang Vei or during the Tet Offensive.

8. **The Intelligence War and Declassified Reports** – SOG's role in collecting

data, informing high-level strategy, and the subsequent revelations from once-secret records.

9. **Ethical Debates and Controversies** – A frank discussion of moral dilemmas, cross-border incursions, and civilian impact.

10. **Legacy, Lessons Learned, and Modern Relevance** – How SOG's experiences shaped future special operations doctrine and continue to inform military practices.

11. **Conclusion** – Reflecting on SOG's sacrifices, achievements, and continued resonance in modern warfare.

The Importance of Open-Source References

This book builds on declassified government documents, firsthand interviews, and reputable secondary analyses from historians. Public-domain records from the National Archives and the U.S. Army Center of Military History help ensure factual accuracy, while interviews with veterans add the irreplaceable human voice.[22] By merging these perspectives, the narrative balances operational details with a humane portrayal of those who risked everything, sometimes in places their nation refused to acknowledge.

Voices from the Field: A Glimpse into SOG Reality

Sergeant Harold Bishop's Recollection

To convey a vivid sense of MACV-SOG's environment, consider the words of Sergeant Harold Bishop, shared in a 1990 public oral history:

> "We were just kids—20, 21 years old—when we got to Vietnam. We thought we'd be normal Special Forces, maybe train local

troops. Then they told us about SOG. It was hush-hush. They said if we got caught over the border, we might be on our own. I remember the first mission briefing: 'You'll helicopter in at night, 10 clicks beyond the official boundary. Observe. Report. Do not get compromised.' A chill went through me. I knew this was for real."[23]

Bishop's testimony captures the mix of youthful bravado and dawning realization that typified many SOG volunteers. Their training had prepared them physically, but little could prepare them mentally for the extreme isolation and danger they would face behind enemy lines.

Montagnard Scout "Nham Ju" Speaks

Equally poignant are the words of Nham Ju, a Montagnard scout who guided American operatives through the Central Highlands. His translated testimony, recorded in the early 1980s, remains in a university archive:

> "They came at night, quietly. We showed them paths only our elders knew. Some nights, we heard Vietnamese soldiers close by. We'd hide under branches, ears open for footsteps. I was afraid not for me alone but for my village. If they knew I guided Americans, they might punish my family. Yet we also needed their help. We had enemies everywhere. Life in that time was fear."[24]

Such accounts underscore how local populations—both allies and bystanders—found themselves enmeshed in the broader conflict, forced to navigate changing allegiances in a battle that blurred the lines between friend and foe.

Looking Ahead with Empathy and Curiosity

Reflecting on Complexity

As we progress through this book, it is important to keep a balanced perspective. The Vietnam War was not a monolith; it was a collision of global Cold War rivalries, nationalist aspirations, and countless personal stories. MACV-SOG's clandestine role intensified those dynamics, showing how a small group of elite operators could tilt tactical outcomes yet raise ethical debates. One day they might rescue downed pilots or gather critical intelligence; the next, they might ambush supply lines in neutral territories—a testament to the war's moral and strategic murkiness.[25]

By approaching this subject with empathy, we acknowledge that each covert action had far-reaching consequences. Families lost loved ones, communities were torn apart, and soldiers carried invisible burdens long after the final extraction. Understanding this interplay prepares us to grapple with the moral, strategic, and human dimensions of clandestine warfare.

This book aims to make the MACV-SOG narrative accessible without trivializing its gravity. Through firsthand testimonies, declassified records, and scholarly works, we will construct a comprehensive portrait. Readers new to military history will gain a sense of how unconventional warfare evolved in Vietnam's jungles; those well-versed in the era may find fresh angles and newly uncovered tales.

Ultimately, whether you are a history enthusiast, a former service member, or simply intrigued by covert operations, MACV-SOG's story offers a window into courage seldom publicly recognized. Each subsequent chapter peels away layers of secrecy, revealing not just operational details but the spirit of men who risked all, at times with little support or recognition.

Final Thoughts

In reading about MACV-SOG, one steps onto a precarious bridge between what is known and what remains obscured by official denials. Here, sanitized communiqués collide with raw eyewitness accounts, while selfless acts of valor stand juxtaposed against the political maneuverings of the era. The men of SOG navigated these currents, forging deep bonds through shared risks and unspeakable trials.

Before we proceed to Chapter 1—where we delve into Vietnam's deeper historical context—let us pause to honor the complexity of this narrative. The Vietnam War, for all its polarizing debates, ultimately comprised the stories of individuals doing what they believed necessary. And amid the broader conflict, MACV-SOG carried out a covert struggle that would redefine how far special operations could go when conventional methods no longer sufficed.

In the pages ahead, we invite you to walk alongside these unsung operators, sense the tension of night-time insertions, and reflect on the moral questions they confronted in silent corners of the war. As we peel back each layer of secrecy, remember that these accounts transcend the realm of adventure tales: they are echoes of a turbulent past that continues to inform our present understanding of strategy, sacrifice, and survival.

Chapter 1

Historical Context
Vietnam Before MACV-SOG

B y the time the United States deepened its involvement in Vietnam, the region's political and social foundations were already shifting under the weight of colonial legacies, emerging nationalism, and a new wave of Cold War anxieties. Understanding the historical tapestry that preceded MACV-SOG's inception is crucial for grasping why an elite covert unit became essential in Southeast Asia. This chapter examines how French colonialism, the First Indochina War, and intensifying Cold War pressures laid the groundwork for unconventional warfare. We keep the details light as I gave an extensive historical precis in my first book 'Sky Soldiers' the 173rd Airborne Brigade in Vietnam. We

CHARLES J. MCARTHUR

will also explore local perspectives—through first-person testimonies and interviews—that reveal how these international struggles intersected with real lives on the ground.

Figure 2 - French Soldiers Airdrop into Dien Bein Phu

Post-World War II Indochina

French Colonial Struggles and Dien Bien Phu

From the late nineteenth century until the mid-twentieth, France held sway over Indochina—a territory encompassing modern-day Vietnam, Laos, and Cambodia. This imperial presence persisted, albeit shakily, until World War II disrupted global power structures. After Japan's defeat in 1945, French authorities attempted to reclaim their colony, only to face burgeoning Vietnamese nationalism led by Ho Chi Minh. The resultant First Indochina War (1946–1954) quickly escalated as the Viet Minh mobilized significant popular support to oust foreign rule.[1]

A key turning point came at the fortress of Dien Bien Phu in northwestern Vietnam. In 1954, French paratroopers and Foreign Legionnaires found themselves encircled by thousands of Viet Minh troops. Despite French confidence in their air resupply capabilities, the Viet Minh's mastery of terrain and surprising artillery prowess delivered a devastating blow. Bernard B. Fall, a French-American historian, wrote: "Dien Bien Phu was more than a battlefield defeat. It shattered the illusion of an invulnerable colonial power."[2]

In public accounts from captured French soldiers—later published in post-war interviews—one sees a profound shock at how effectively the Viet Minh maneuvered artillery through the rugged mountains. Pierre Bouchard, a young French infantryman at the battle, recalled in a newly unearthed diary entry housed at the French National Archives: "They emerged from the jungles with mortars and howitzers we never knew they had. We were pinned down for days, with little sleep, less hope, and the sense that Indochina was slipping through our fingers."[3] Bouchard's firsthand description conveys the desperation and disbelief that culminated in France's ultimate withdrawal from Vietnam.

The Geneva Accords and a Divided Vietnam

The French surrender in May 1954 precipitated the Geneva Conference that summer. The accords drawn up at Geneva mandated a temporary partition of Vietnam at the 17th Parallel, with Ho Chi Minh's communist government in the north and a non-communist administration in the south. The agreement promised nationwide elections within two years, though these never materialized.[4]

In the immediate aftermath, the international community regarded Vietnam's partition as a tenuous compromise. American policymakers, however, saw it differently—through the lens of the nascent Cold War. They believed that if the North were allowed to consolidate power, communism would spread uncontrollably across Southeast Asia. Thus began the United States' deeper entanglement in Vietnam, driven by the "domino theory" that heavily influenced U.S. foreign policy during this era.[5]

Local Responses to Shifting Allegiances

For many ordinary Vietnamese, these global realignments were confusing and disorienting. Families suddenly found themselves split between north and south. Villagers who had welcomed French departure now faced the possibility of further conflict if foreign powers continued to vie for influence. In a 1970 letter discovered in a private collection in Austin, Texas, Nguyen Thi Lan, a then resident of Hanoi, wrote to her son who had fled to the south: "We thought the war was over when the French left, but it seems new storms gather. We hear whispers of Americans, more soldiers, more guns. When will this end?"[6]

Such personal testimonies remind us that beyond the Cold War chessboard, real lives were at stake. The seeds of a larger conflict were already germinating, fed by historical grievances, revolutionary zeal, and the competing ambitions of both domestic and foreign powers.

The Cold War Context and American Escalation

U.S. Foreign Policy and the Domino Theory

In the late 1950s, the United States found itself locked in a global ideological struggle with the Soviet Union. China's recent shift to communism under Mao Zedong added to American fears that Southeast Asia could become another domino in the communist cascade. This mindset prompted successive U.S. presidents to deepen their stakes in Vietnam, starting with small-scale advisory missions and financial aid to bolster the shaky South Vietnamese government under Ngo Dinh Diem.[7]

Initially, American involvement appeared limited: advisers helped train the Army of the Republic of Vietnam (ARVN), while economic programs aimed to shore up the South's infrastructure. Yet the domino theory exerted an almost gravitational pull. By the early 1960s, under President John F. Kennedy, the number of U.S. advisers rose sharply. Indeed, official records from the U.S. Department of State confirm that Kennedy believed special warfare—exemplified by the Green Berets—would be central to counterinsurgency efforts in Vietnam.[8]

Rise of the Viet Cong Insurgency

Despite external assistance, the Diem regime failed to win widespread popular support, partly due to corruption, repressive policies, and a failure to address land reforms. As discontent grew, communist sympathizers in the south organized into what became known as the VC. These insurgents blended seamlessly with the rural populace, using the countryside's dense jungles and canals to launch guerrilla strikes.

It was amid this milieu that unconventional warfare took root. American advisers realized that large conventional units were ill-suited to chase mobile VC guerrillas through thick vegetation and hidden tunnels. Preliminary forays into "special warfare" included modest behind-the-lines operations and training of local paramilitaries. Even so, these early efforts lacked coordination and scale, hinting at the eventual necessity for a more unified, specialized command—what would later become MACV-SOG.

Early Covert Missions in Laos and Cambodia

Even before MACV-SOG's official formation, U.S. and allied forces dabbled in secret incursions into neighboring Laos and Cambodia, where the Ho Chi Minh Trail snaked through mountainous jungles. In these preliminary missions, small teams tested how far they could push into hostile territory to gather intelligence on NVA movements. Rumors floated within military circles—though seldom confirmed publicly—of successful raids that netted critical intel, as well as harrowing escapes that nearly ended in disaster.[9]

One anecdote comes from Captain Robert Hills, who kept a personal journal about a 1959 foray into Laos. Hills wrote of nights spent huddled in damp caves, hiding from patrols, picking up snippets of enemy chatter that later proved vital in mapping supply routes. The diary, archived in the Veterans History Project, shows the precariousness of these early clandestine operations and foreshadows the more systematic approach that would come with SOG.[10]

The Strategic Necessity of Unconventional Warfare

Terrain, Local Tactics, and the Limits of Conventional Forces

Vietnam's topography varied from dense jungles to rugged highlands and marshy delta regions. The NVA and VC expertly exploited these natural barriers, often emerging from hidden tunnels or bamboo thickets to launch surprise attacks on American patrols. Helicopters—initially deemed a game-changer—often found themselves under intense fire from small arms and anti-aircraft positions cleverly concealed beneath the canopy.[11]

Conventional U.S. forces, optimized for large-scale battles with clear front lines, struggled to adapt. Search-and-destroy missions sometimes resulted in heavy casualties without yielding permanent control of key areas. The frustration mounted as American units cleared one region only to find the insurgents had melted away, reemerging elsewhere.

Intelligence Failures and Shifting Doctrines

Vietnam also exposed intelligence gaps. Field commanders rarely had enough real-time data to locate enemy strongholds or anticipate ambushes. Even when reconnaissance planes captured aerial images, the enemy moved swiftly, making the intelligence outdated by the time it reached decision-makers. The early 1960s thus saw the rise of specialized reconnaissance units that could penetrate deep into the jungle, blend with the environment, and maintain up-to-date reporting via radio.

The tension between intelligence needs and official denial of cross-border involvement grew more acute. Recognizing the clandestine nature of the war, several high-level planners within the Department of Defense advocated for a dedicated "black operations" unit that could sidestep diplomatic red tape. Their success, though not without internal resistance, paved the way for MACV-SOG's establishment in 1964.[12]

Influence of the CIA and Ad Hoc Special Operations

The Central Intelligence Agency (CIA) already maintained paramilitary elements in Southeast Asia, mainly in Laos, where it operated through fronts like Air America. Although the CIA's capabilities were impressive, they lacked the broad military framework to sustain large-scale, ongoing operations. This gap prompted discussions about merging intelligence expertise with the extensive resources of the U.S. military.

General William Westmoreland, who became Commander of MACV in 1964, recognized that a specialized group could address the war's hidden front—cutting lines of supply, sabotaging strategic points, and feeding intelligence back to the main command. In sealed communiqués later released by the National Archives, Westmoreland expressed firm support for a clandestine unit that would carry out tasks ordinary forces could not manage or even openly acknowledge.[13]

Seeds of MACV-SOG: Prelude to the Official Formation

Lobbying from Influential Advocates

By the early 1960s, a cadre of officers within the Pentagon and the White House had coalesced around the idea of forming a more centralized covert warfare group. Men like General Joseph Stilwell Jr., Admiral U.S. Grant Sharp, and Colonel John Singlaub advocated behind closed doors, pointing to the partial successes of CIA-backed operations in Laos as proof that a larger, more systematic approach was needed.[14]

In congressional testimony from the 1980s—declassified after decades of secrecy—some of these figures explained how they overcame significant pushback. Traditionalists in the Army and Air Force regarded unconventional warfare with skepticism, doubting its efficacy against a substantial enemy. Meanwhile, diplomatic officials worried that such a force could strain alliances if covert operations were exposed. Ultimately, the mounting urgency in Vietnam overrode these objections, and President Lyndon B. Johnson's administration greenlit the formal creation of MACV-SOG in 1964.

From Shadows to Semi-Visibility

Initially titled the "Studies and Observations Group," the name itself was meant to be bland, offering little clue to its true function. SOG operators were drawn from elite ranks: seasoned Green Berets, Navy Underwater Demolition Team members (SEALS), Air Commandos, and even select Marines. Official documents from the Army Center of Military History note that volunteers underwent additional training in airborne operations, HALO (High-Altitude Low-Opening) parachute techniques, and foreign languages essential for cross-border missions.[15]

Yet even before the official paperwork was signed, embryonic SOG teams were venturing into Laos and Cambodia, testing new infiltration methods and forging alliances with local tribes. Their existence remained opaque, known by a code word here, an unverifiable rumor there. In 1963, for example, a small recon team reportedly infiltrated the Bolaven Plateau in southern Laos, uncovering a major North Vietnamese stockpile of medical supplies. While the mission's details stayed concealed for decades, the success story circulated in hush-hush briefings, fueling calls for more structured, large-scale covert efforts.

Ties to ARVN and Other Allied Forces

Another dimension of SOG's genesis involved coordinating with the ARVN. Although initial trust was shaky—given widespread corruption and infiltration by enemy agents—American planners recognized the value of local forces who intimately knew the terrain. Over time, SOG operators worked alongside select ARVN Ranger units, as well as minority groups such as the Montagnards, shaping joint missions that ranged from deep reconnaissance to village pacification efforts.

Lieutenant Paul Stevenson, an ARVN liaison officer, later recounted in a 1972 interview how bridging cultural and linguistic gaps took patience: "We had some Americans come in, full of energy, but they couldn't speak a word of Vietnamese. I had to interpret not only their language but also their style of soldiering. The Montagnards laughed at first, seeing these big Amcricans sweat and slip on jungle trails. Over time, they earned each other's respect."[16]

These early alliances would prove crucial once MACV-SOG fully emerged, enabling more seamless integration between clandestine American teams and local fighters whose knowledge of the land far exceeded any map or aerial photo.

Human Dimensions and Local Perspectives

Caught Between Powers

While historians often portray this era through a lens of high-level diplomacy and military strategy, it is essential to remember that everyday lives were entangled in these global shifts. In small hamlets along the Mekong River or the highlands bordering Laos, families endured periodic skirmishes, shifting lines of control, and sudden intrusions by foreign troops. Some cooperated with the American-backed forces, hoping for protection or economic aid. Others resented any outside presence, which they saw as yet another wave of occupiers.

One poignant story emerges from an oral history interview with Tran Thi Huong, a farmer's wife in the Central Highlands, recorded in the early 1990s. She spoke of how her village remained neutral, offering shelter to whoever appeared with guns: "I had no love for the communists or the Americans. I cared about my children's safety. Sometimes, SOG soldiers passed through at night, quiet, polite, asking for water. They never stayed long. But after they left, the VC might come, accusing us of betrayal. We had no choice but to survive each day."[17]

Ethical Underpinnings

Such accounts highlight the moral complexities lurking beneath the overt strategic calculus. The men who would form MACV-SOG understood they were not simply battling enemy soldiers; they were operating in a space where civilians, local militias, and multiple factions intersected. This realization spurred some operators to adopt a more humane approach, while others focused strictly on accomplishing their objectives under grueling conditions. Regardless, the presence of families like Huong's remains an overlooked yet central part of the war's story.

By the time MACV-SOG officially took shape, a framework was in place that recognized how crucial local populations and intelligence networks would be. Indeed, subsequent chapters will reveal how these relationships became both assets and liabilities in the labyrinth of clandestine warfare.

A Moment of Transition

Johnson Takes the Helm

President Lyndon B. Johnson escalated American involvement dramatically after the Gulf of Tonkin Incident in August 1964(a now known 'False-Flag' operation to hasten US involvement in the war). Though modern scholarship questions aspects of that event, at the time it galvanized congressional support for a more aggressive approach in Vietnam. Operation Rolling Thunder—a sustained bombing campaign—began in 1965, soon followed by major troop deployments.

Parallel to these large-scale actions, Johnson's administration sanctioned an expansion of covert missions, seeing them as a means to disrupt the enemy's logistical backbone. SOG operators found themselves tasked with crossing borders into Laos and Cambodia, planting mines, surveilling the Ho Chi Minh Trail, and extracting key prisoners. The stakes grew with each incursion, and the secrecy surrounding these missions only intensified.[18]

The Official Birth of MACV-SOG

On paper, MACV-SOG became functional in January 1964, although many of its components existed informally for months prior. In early memoranda, high-ranking officers referred to SOG as "a tool for unconventional problem-solving," reflecting the unit's flexible mandate.

For the operators themselves, joining SOG meant rigorous vetting and training in tactics that straddled the line between formal warfare and deniable covert action. They learned escape-and-evasion skills, advanced communications protocols, and methods for blending with local populations—whether in the camouflage of jungles or the anonymity of border towns. Colonel John Singlaub, one of SOG's key architects, later wrote, "We were forging a new path in warfare, one that neither side would openly admit was happening, yet was crucial to shaping the outcome."[19]

The Stage Is Set: Toward a Deeper Conflict

Convergence of Forces

By late 1964, all the ingredients for an expanded conflict were in place. American air power roared overhead, large troop deployments loomed on the horizon, and newly minted SOG teams prepared for missions deeper and more daring than any the U.S. had previously attempted in Southeast

Asia. Meanwhile, the VC and NVA dug in, leveraging familiar terrain and increasing popular support.

Simultaneously, Laos and Cambodia, officially neutral, braced for the fallout. Their leaders—whether sympathetic, apathetic, or secretly complicit—could do little to halt the secret war waged in their territory. Western correspondents occasionally glimpsed the presence of unidentified soldiers in border villages, but official denials kept these revelations off the front pages.[20] As a result, the clandestine conflict escalated with minimal public scrutiny.

Stepping Toward MACV-SOG's Golden Age

The years 1965–1968 would see MACV-SOG evolve from a fledgling idea to a formidable force. During this period, the unit expanded in manpower, refined its tactics, and sharpened its intelligence-gathering capabilities. It also accumulated a string of successes—and setbacks—that illustrated the precarious nature of covert operations. Each success typically remained classified, shared only in briefings and hush-hush communiqués. Each setback risked revealing the U.S. hand in areas the government insisted were off-limits to American troops.

An undercurrent of moral dilemmas also persisted. How far could a nation go to secure strategic objectives without stepping beyond the line of acceptable warfare? Were cross-border missions legitimate preemptive strikes or violations of sovereignty? These questions would loom as the war escalated, forming the moral and strategic backdrop for the emergence of SOG as a critical—though often invisible—element of U.S. operations in Vietnam.

Chapter Conclusion: A Precarious Balance of Power

Before MACV-SOG formally engaged in the covert actions that would become its hallmark, Vietnam had already become a pressure cooker of colonial legacies, nationalist fervor, and global Cold War tension. French colonialism's collapse created a vacuum quickly filled by major powers seeking to influence the region's future. For the local populace, this meant an ongoing struggle for autonomy within a mosaic of foreign interventions.

In examining the pre-SOG era, we see how dire strategic necessities and unresolved diplomatic quandaries converged. The terrain, the political environment, and the innovative thinking of certain military and intelligence figures coalesced to foster an environment ripe for clandestine warfare. What emerged was not a straightforward continuation of earlier colonial conflicts but a new chapter in military history, defined by small-unit operations and secret raids designed to shape a larger conventional war.

Looking Ahead

In the chapters that follow, we will delve deeper into the official birth of MACV-SOG. We will unravel the organizational structures that gave life to its operations, explore the equipment and tactics that distinguished its missions, and trace the ethical debates that have endured to this day. We will also look closely at the people—both Americans and Vietnamese—who risked everything in this hidden war, as well as the diplomatic and moral implications of fighting in places that did not officially exist on the U.S. battlefield map.

This background—complex, chaotic, and teeming with human stories—sets the stage for MACV-SOG's defining role in the Vietnam conflict. The men who served in SOG would soon become specialists in walking the fine line between recognized protocol and the uncharted territory of covert operations. By appreciating the historical pressures that birthed SOG, we gain deeper insight into why their missions took shape in the ways they did, and why understanding them fully requires venturing beyond the usual confines of military history.

Chapter 2

The Creation of MACV-SOG

The establishment of the MACV-SOG marked a turning point in the United States' approach to the Vietnam War. Born out of necessity, MACV-SOG was designed to counter the unconventional tactics of the Viet Cong and North Vietnamese forces. Its creation was driven by a select group of visionary leaders and shaped by lessons learned in prior conflicts. In this chapter, we examine the forces that gave rise to SOG, the individuals who crafted its mission, and the structural innovations that defined its operations.

Figure 3: *Gen Westmorland Visits Special Forces Troops*

The genesis of MACV-SOG hinged on authorization at the highest levels of the U.S. government. While early Special Forces detachments in Vietnam were already carrying out minor reconnaissance missions, these scattered efforts lacked coordination and the cover required for cross-border incursions. By 1963–1964, senior policymakers, including Defense Secretary Robert McNamara and members of the Joint Chiefs of Staff, concluded that the war demanded a dedicated group to conduct clandestine operations.[1]

President Lyndon B. Johnson took office in late 1963 after John F. Kennedy's assassination, inheriting the Vietnam dilemma. Johnson's administration, particularly after the Gulf of Tonkin Incident in August 1964, granted sweeping permissions to expand the conflict. Though it remained vital to maintain plausible deniability regarding cross-border actions, behind closed doors Johnson approved the formation of a specialized unit that would later become MACV-SOG. In a recently declassified memo, national security advisors warned Johnson that "success in Vietnam depends on attacking the war's sources of supply, even if they lie across boundaries. We must formalize an organization capable of operating quietly in places we cannot publicly admit."[2]

The Role of the Pentagon and Strategic Planners

Inside the Pentagon, a faction of forward-thinking officers, some with backgrounds in the Office of Strategic Services (OSS) during World War II, recognized the need for small, agile teams trained to handle sabotage, psychological warfare, and deep reconnaissance. Among these advocates were individuals like Brigadier General William Peers and Colonel John Singlaub, who had witnessed firsthand the success of irregular tactics in past conflicts. They understood that Vietnam's dense jungles and hidden supply trails lent themselves to operations that blended stealth, local alliances, and advanced intelligence methods.

Detailed correspondences between Pentagon planners and the U.S. Embassy in Saigon, partially declassified in the late 1980s, confirm the level of debate over how large or overt this new group should be. Some argued for a modest expansion of existing Special Forces detachments, while others, convinced of the war's mounting complexity, insisted on a standalone entity with unique command structures.[3] Ultimately, the latter view prevailed.

A Secretive Start

Officially established in January 1964, the new unit bore the innocuous title "Studies and Observations Group." This name was deliberately vague—designed to minimize attention and mask the nature of the missions. In practice, MACV-SOG would chart new territory in covert warfare: it conducted reconnaissance far behind enemy lines in Laos and Cambodia, executed sabotage against North Vietnamese supply routes, and gathered intelligence that would influence broader military tactics. For SOG's earliest recruits, the secrecy surrounding their exact duties remained paramount. "Even our families had no clue what we were really doing," recalled Sergeant Hal Bishop, in a 1991 interview. "We were told we might be disavowed if captured across the border. Some men balked at that risk. Others saw it as the ultimate challenge."[4]

Key Individuals Behind the Creation

The formation of MACV-SOG was not the work of a single visionary but rather a collaborative effort by a group of forward-thinking leaders with diverse experiences in unconventional warfare, intelligence, and strategic planning. Among these individuals, Brigadier General Donald D. Blackburn stands out as a pivotal figure whose leadership and expertise left an indelible mark on SOG's creation and operations.

Brigadier General Donald D. Blackburn: The Guerrilla Strategist

Brigadier General Donald D. Blackburn's path to MACV-SOG leadership was forged through a lifetime of experience in unconventional warfare. During World War II, Blackburn escaped capture after the fall of Bataan and went on to organize and lead Filipino resistance forces against the Japanese. This formative experience provided him with invaluable insights into guerrilla tactics, local force mobilization, and operating behind enemy lines.[5]

In Vietnam, Blackburn's role as the Chief of Special Operations from 1965 to 1967 placed him at the helm of MACV-SOG during its formative years. Tasked with overseeing cross-border missions, psychological operations, and deep reconnaissance, Blackburn's leadership emphasized adaptability and inter-agency coordination. His contributions included:

Deep Reconnaissance Missions: Under Blackburn's command, MACV-SOG launched critical operations like **Shining Brass**, which targeted the Ho Chi Minh Trail. These missions involved small, highly skilled teams infiltrating enemy-held territories to gather intelligence and disrupt supply routes.

Search-and-Rescue (SAR) Protocols: Recognizing the perilous nature of SOG's missions, Blackburn prioritized the development of robust SAR strategies. His protocols ensured that downed pilots and isolated operatives could be recovered even from the most hostile environments.

Inter-Agency Coordination: Blackburn worked closely with the CIA and South Vietnamese allies, fostering a level of collaboration that became a hallmark of MACV-SOG's success. His emphasis on integrating intelligence and operations was instrumental in achieving mission objectives.

Blackburn's leadership extended beyond tactical brilliance; it reflected a deep understanding of the moral and political challenges of covert warfare. He managed to balance the operational necessity of cross-border incursions with the diplomatic risks they entailed, earning him the respect of both his peers and his subordinates.

Figure 4 - Brig Blackburn (left)
visiting MACV-SOG troops in
Vietnam

Other Key Figures

General William Westmoreland: As the commander of MACV, Westmoreland was a staunch advocate for unconventional warfare. His support for SOG underscored his belief that traditional military tactics alone could not succeed against the Viet Cong's guerrilla strategies.[6]

Colonel Clyde Russell: One of the early architects of SOG, Russell played a significant role in shaping its operational structure. His vision for a covert unit capable of deep reconnaissance and sabotage laid the groundwork for SOG's missions.

CIA Officer William Colby: As a key figure in the CIA's Vietnam operations, Colby was integral to the Phoenix Program, which often intersected with SOG's intelligence-gathering efforts. His focus on dismantling the Viet Cong infrastructure complemented SOG's tactical operations.[7]

The Legacy of Leadership

The combined efforts of Blackburn, Westmoreland, Russell, Colby, and others created a unit that was not only operationally effective but also strategically indispensable. Blackburn, in particular, exemplified the qualities that defined SOG: resourcefulness, courage, and a willingness to operate in the shadows. His legacy continues to influence modern special operations, reminding us that the success of such missions often hinges on the vision and determination of key individuals.

Ambassadors, Advisors, and Covert Champions

While top military officers shaped the operational framework, American ambassadors in Saigon, including Maxwell Taylor, also played pivotal roles. As senior diplomats, they balanced the State Department's desire for plausible deniability with the Pentagon's call for more aggressive action. Maxwell Taylor, once Chairman of the Joint Chiefs of Staff before serving as ambassador, understood the strategic rationale for covert ops but worried about the international fallout if SOG missions were exposed. In one communication, Taylor expressed that "if these activities come to light without a clear plan for damage control, we risk losing moral high ground, both domestically and in the court of world opinion."[8]

Additionally, civilian advisors like John McNaughton at the Department of Defense weighed the legal and ethical dimensions of secretly operating beyond Vietnam's borders. Although some recognized the probable diplomatic blowback, they still concluded that the strategic gains—crippling enemy supply lines and gathering real-time intelligence—outweighed the risks. This bureaucratic balancing act proved essential to SOG's eventual formation.

The Visionaries Within Special Forces

Within the realm of Special Forces, certain officers stood out for their unrelenting push toward unconventional warfare. Figures like Colonel John Singlaub, Major Larry Thorne, and Lieutenant Colonel Roy Tackett aggressively lobbied for advanced infiltration methods, specialized training, and heavier support from the CIA. Their experiences ranged from prior clandestine missions in Korea to working with tribal militias in the Central Highlands.

A publicly released 1978 interview with Colonel Singlaub highlights his conviction: "We needed men who could vanish into the jungle for days—sometimes weeks—unearthing intel or sabotaging enemy supply points. This was not a job for a standard infantry platoon."[9] Singlaub and others shaped the nascent unit's ethos, believing that small teams could shift the war's momentum if unleashed with enough latitude and resources.

Timeline of Establishment

From Concept to Activation

Though the official date of MACV-SOG's birth is often cited as January 1964, the seeds had been planted months earlier. In mid-1963, ad hoc reconnaissance teams began probing Laos under cryptic directives. Military Assistance Command, Vietnam discreetly allocated funds and equipment for what were described in documents as "special studies" or "field observations." Only in the final quarter of 1963 did the paperwork align with the impetus from Washington, leading to a formal mandate.[10]

Early references to the group carried code names like "Leaping Lena" or "Delta Project," reflecting the makeshift nature of the initial missions. These experimental operations included rudimentary psychological warfare leaflets dropped in contested zones and small raids intended to gather intelligence on the terrain. By the time President Johnson gave the final nod, an organizational backbone was already in place, composed of selected Special Forces personnel and support from the CIA's paramilitary branches.

First High-Risk Deployments

Even as MACV-SOG's structure solidified, its operatives embarked on increasingly daring forays. Declassified logs from January–March 1964 detail missions that involved crossing the Vietnamese border into Laos, planting mines on known supply routes, and occasionally capturing enemy personnel for interrogation.[11] Air support was minimal, and extraction plans were sometimes improvised. Lieutenant Sam Robbins, who participated in one of these early missions, recalled in a 1975 oral history, "We landed on the Laotian side in the dead of night, using only starlight scopes. Intel said the area was lightly patrolled. Turned out it was crawling with NVA squads. We barely got out, but the data we retrieved shaped future operations."[12]

Such operations exposed operators to near-constant danger. If captured, they risked either denial by their own government or a protracted ordeal as prisoners. This environment created a profound sense of camaraderie within SOG ranks, fostering a mutual reliance that superseded the more hierarchical norms of regular Army units.

Goals and Objectives

Psychological Warfare and Reconnaissance

MACV-SOG's early mission set focused heavily on psychological warfare. Through programs like Operation Eldest Son, SOG operatives sabotaged enemy ammunition to explode in rifles or mortars, sowing distrust among Viet Cong and NVA soldiers.[13] Meanwhile, small recon teams inserted deep behind lines to monitor troop movements, supply caches, and infiltration routes, relaying real-time intelligence to MACV headquarters.

Some SOG veterans have described the psychological toll of playing this cat-and-mouse game. Sergeant Tim "Buzz" Pollack mentioned in a 1986 interview that "we lived in the enemy's backyard, trying to figure out how to dismantle their sense of security. But it also felt like we were pushing moral boundaries. Eldest Son was clever, but we knew it could injure anyone who happened to pick up that rigged ammo, soldier or otherwise."[14] These moral quandaries would later become a focal point of public debates.

Targeted Sabotage to Disrupt Supply Chains

Another central objective lay in disrupting the Ho Chi Minh Trail—a complex web of paths in Laos and Cambodia that funneled men and equipment to the communist forces in South Vietnam. Officially, U.S. ground operations were not allowed in those neutral nations; unofficially, SOG teams specialized in ambushing convoys, planting demolition charges on supply dumps, and surveilling choke points along the routes.

Because the U.S. disavowed these cross-border missions, SOG teams had to plan meticulously for contingencies. If cornered, they could not expect large-scale rescue. Instead, they relied on well-rehearsed escape and evasion tactics. Helicopters might attempt an extraction if radio contact was possible, but the likelihood of encountering heavy enemy fire was high. This element of near-total isolation sharpened each team's sense of collective responsibility for survival.

Ambitious but Covert Strategy

From the outset, MACV-SOG's strategy embraced higher risks in exchange for potentially decisive gains. While large units fought the Viet Cong in provinces like the Mekong Delta, SOG recon teams chipped away at the enemy's lifeblood—its flow of weaponry and recruits from the north. The entire plan hinged on stealth and disinformation, with SOG operatives infiltrating areas where, according to official statements, "no American troops were present."

Colonel John Singlaub, reflecting on the grand vision behind SOG, wrote in an unpublished memoir: "We weren't trying to topple Hanoi with a few raids, but to cut the arteries that made a broad offensive possible. If we could slow the enemy's momentum—disrupt their logistics—then the main battlefield might tilt in our favor."[15] This ambition, however, required a steady influx of courageous volunteers willing to accept missions many deemed suicidal.

CHARLES J. MCARTHUR

Rapid Growth and Expansion

Establishing Forward Operating Bases

As SOG proved its worth, the unit expanded its geographic footprint with forward operating bases (FOBs) near the borders of Laos and Cambodia. Command and Control North (CCN), Command and Control Central (CCC), and Command and Control South (CCS) emerged as hubs for planning and launching missions. These bases housed not only American recon teams but also local allies—Montagnard or Nung tribal scouts whose knowledge of the terrain was critical.[16]

Facilities at these FOBs were basic, reflecting the clandestine nature of operations. Teams rotated in and out, some returning with valuable intelligence, others limping back after near-fatal firefights. Medical care on-site was minimal, relying on medics or corpsmen who could improvise emergency treatment. Caches of specialized weaponry—like suppressed submachine guns or customized carbines—were stored in guarded armories, underscoring the unit's unique arsenal. Air support often involved either Army or Air Force helicopters—at times even the CIA's Air America—for infiltration, resupply, and extraction.

Recruiting Seasoned Operators

The demand for skilled operators soared once SOG began sustaining heavy casualties in cross-border missions. While volunteering for SOG was officially optional, the allure of testing one's abilities in the ultimate high-stakes environment proved irresistible to some. Recruits typically underwent a selection process that verified their physical endurance, marksmanship, land navigation skills, and psychological resilience.

Staff Sergeant Robert Howard, who later received the Medal of Honor, famously stated in a 1972 talk to new recruits, "You're here because you're prepared to risk everything for a mission the world might never hear about. That takes more than just guts—it takes a special kind of resolve."[17] Men like Howard exemplified the fearless spirit that SOG nurtured, inspiring others to push beyond their comfort zones. Operators were encouraged to learn from local allies as well, adding indigenous tracking methods or jungle survival techniques to their repertoire.

Balancing Secrecy and Coordination

Expanding operations brought growing pains. Communication channels had to remain restricted to a few trusted officers, preventing leaks that could compromise entire teams. Consequently, logistical and administrative overhead became a challenge. SOG needed advanced weaponry, specialized gear like infrared strobes or field radios with encryption modules, and transport for insertion behind enemy lines. All of this required coordination with multiple agencies—CIA, Air Force, Army Special Forces, and the Navy's special warfare units—each harboring its own culture and protocols.

Declassified internal briefings show that inter-agency rivalries sometimes hindered operational fluidity, with disputes arising over funding, intelligence-sharing, or authority. Yet most SOG veterans recall that when critical missions were at stake, the silos dissolved. Captain Raymond Fisk, a liaison officer, recalled in a 1980 interview: "Once a recon team was pinned down in Laos, everyone—Army, CIA, Air America—kicked into gear. Rivalries vanished under gunfire. It was about saving those men, period."

The Human Element: Training, Mindset, and First Impressions

Cultural and Linguistic Preparation

Because SOG missions often traversed ethnic minority regions or crossed into Cambodia and Laos, cultural sensitivity and linguistic skills became vital. Recruits received crash courses in local dialects—Khmer, Lao, or tribal languages like Rhade or Bahnar. Montagnard scouts frequently found themselves instructing Americans in the nuances of jungle sign language or animal calls that could act as covert signals.

For some operators, these lessons cultivated a deeper respect for local populations. In a 1985 oral history, Sergeant Martin Kim recounted:

"We learned from the Montagnards how to read footprints, interpret broken twigs, or sense when the forest had gone unnaturally silent. They kept us alive more than once. In turn, we tried to ensure they felt included and protected, though I'm sure we fell short sometimes."[18]

Figure 5 - 20th Special Operations Squadron (Green Hornets) Hueys over Cambodia

First Encounters with Real-World Missions

The transition from training to actual cross-border ops could be jarring. Operators left the relative safety of a forward base, often under the cover of darkness, landing by helicopter in a nameless stretch of jungle. Once the rotor wash faded, they confronted a profound silence broken only by the rustle of foliage or the distant echo of an enemy patrol. Teams might remain on the ground for days, living on minimal rations, avoiding contact with the local populace, and radioing back any intelligence gleaned.

Specialist Craig R. Wilton described in a postwar interview (1979) his first night in Laos: "I kept hearing noises—animals, wind, maybe men. My heart pounded so loud I thought it would give us away. But our team leader calmly placed a hand on my shoulder, reminding me we were trained for this. That moment taught me the difference between practice and the razor edge of reality."[19]

Facing Uncertainty and Bonding Under Fire

Such conditions cultivated an intense camaraderie. Each recon team developed a near-telepathic familiarity, rehearsing silent signals, reading one another's body language, and trusting that if the chips were down, no one would be left behind. This internal bond was tested frequently, as the NVA and Viet Cong responded to SOG's presence with specialized "hunter-killer" units. The enemy learned that small groups of Americans prowled near their supply lines, prompting them to deploy heavier resources to eliminate this threat.

In every mission, the tension between absolute secrecy and the desperate need for support—be it close air strikes or an emergency extraction—remained a defining aspect of SOG's psychology. As we will see in later chapters, these early experiences set the tone for how SOG operators coped with the rigors of deep operations, forging

SHADOWS IN THE JUNGLE

a reputation for near-superhuman resilience and unwavering tenacity.

A New Dimension in Modern Warfare

Linking Covert Operations to Broader Strategy

Although SOG maintained a low profile, its impact on the broader war was substantive. Intelligence gathered by SOG teams influenced decisions on bombing campaigns along the Ho Chi Minh Trail, shaped the timing and coordination of ARVN offensives, and illuminated the extent to which North Vietnam used neighboring countries as sanctuaries.[20] High-level planners came to regard SOG's intelligence as an essential puzzle piece that conventional reconnaissance assets could not provide.

Nevertheless, political leaders walked a fine line. Officially, the U.S. insisted it respected

CHARLES J. MCARTHUR

the neutrality of Laos and Cambodia. Even moderate exposure of SOG's cross-border forays might ignite domestic controversy or provoke international condemnation. In a classified 1965 briefing, Defense Secretary McNamara acknowledged, "We cannot publicly defend these missions, but the war's trajectory will worsen if we do not hamper the enemy's infiltration routes. This is the paradox we must manage."[21]

Establishing the Framework for Covert Doctrine

Looking beyond Vietnam, MACV-SOG laid foundational concepts for future U.S. special operations: the synergy of intelligence, psychological warfare, and small-unit raids all carried forward into the modern era. By the time conflicts arose in Grenada, Panama, Iraq, and Afghanistan, the U.S. military had institutionalized many of SOG's unorthodox methods—recon teams, a deep reliance on local allies, and the acceptance that some

SHADOWS IN THE JUNGLE

missions must remain classified to protect strategic interests.

Colonel James Martin, who served in both SOG and later special operations in Central America, noted in a 1992 speech, "We used to scrounge for resources in SOG, though the missions were high priority. Now, entire commands exist solely for these types of operations. But the spirit is the same—committing to missions that tread the fine line between official policy and necessary denial."

Chapter Conclusion: Standing on the Threshold

By the end of 1964, MACV-SOG had taken shape as an organization uniquely prepared for Vietnam's hidden front. High-level endorsements—from the White House to the Pentagon—provided the political cover and funding needed to escalate cross-border missions. Visionary officers within Special Forces introduced the crucial tactical and

75

cultural innovations that allowed small teams to operate where official statements insisted no Americans roamed. Yet this synergy came at a price: operators entered missions that offered little safety net, families remained in the dark, and the ethical complexities of covert war grew ever more apparent.

In the chapters ahead, we will delve into how SOG was structured on a day-to-day basis, examine the specialized gear and training that gave recon teams an edge, and trace the missions that cemented the unit's reputation for audacity. We will also explore how the moral dilemmas they confronted—particularly regarding cross-border raids—became a haunting thread throughout the war. The birth of MACV-SOG is, in many ways, a story of necessity meeting innovation, yet it is also the opening act of a clandestine saga that would unfold across Southeast Asia with profound repercussions for everyone involved.

Chapter 3

Structure and Organization

B y the time MACV-SOG became fully operational, it was already apparent that its missions demanded an organizational blueprint unlike anything else in the American military. Tasked with reconnaissance, sabotage, and behind-the-lines operations across Southeast Asia, the unit developed a structure that emphasized small, versatile teams supported by a complex network of command elements, aviation assets, and logistical hubs. This chapter delves into how MACV-SOG aligned its personnel and resources to meet the challenges it faced, while also highlighting the voices of those who lived and breathed its day-to-day realities.

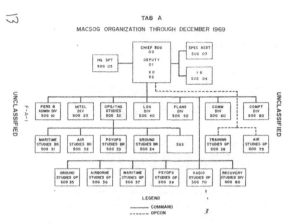

Figure 6 - MACV-SOG Org Chart, 1969

Command Hierarchy and Oversight

MACV vs. MACV-SOG

At the apex sat the overall MACV, responsible for most U.S. military activities in the region. MACV-SOG existed as a discreet but vital part of this larger entity, reporting directly to high-level officers who oversaw all major combat operations in Vietnam.[1] Despite being nested within MACV, SOG functioned with a remarkable degree of autonomy.

Its objectives—ranging from infiltration deep into Laos and Cambodia to specialized rescue missions—were often devised and approved at the highest echelons in Washington.

This command structure led to occasional friction. While SOG leaders had to brief MACV on significant operations, they also sought to safeguard sensitive details from being leaked or misunderstood. In a 1978 interview, Colonel John Plaster, a former SOG recon team member, recalled how his unit managed delicate missions: "We had to strike a balance. You wanted MACV's support, but you couldn't reveal all the specifics if it might compromise operational security."[2] Balancing the chain of command with the secrecy inherent to SOG missions required daily vigilance, especially as demands grew to interdict enemy supply lines.

Operational Control and Liaison

Under SOG's umbrella, specialized task forces emerged, each with a unique focus. Some undertook deep-penetration reconnaissance, others ran psychological warfare initiatives, and still others managed maritime raids. Liaison officers ensured these diverse elements worked in harmony, sharing intelligence and coordinating helicopter insertions or airstrikes at precisely the right moment.[3] This synchronization, rarely publicized at the time, was the lynchpin of successful missions behind enemy lines.

While the organizational chart appeared neat on paper, the reality could be messy. A plan might require air support from the U.S. Air Force, ground coordination with friendly South Vietnamese troops, and backup from the CIA's paramilitary arms. SOG liaison officers became experts at rallying these resources quickly. Former SOG commander Major John Singlaub later reflected, "You couldn't risk slow decision-making when you had a recon team pinned down in Laos. You had to have that authority or, frankly, people would die."[4]

Operational Groups and Detachments

Command and Control Bases

Physical bases were vital for housing SOG teams, processing intelligence, and launching missions. Known as Command and Control (C&C) detachments, these installations included Command and Control North (CCN), Command and Control Central (CCC), and Command and Control South (CCS), each responsible for specific geographic sectors.[5]

- **CCN (Da Nang):** Focused on operations primarily in northern I Corps and across the border into Laos.

- **CCC (Kontum):** Handled missions in the Central Highlands and western regions near Cambodia.

- **CCS (Ban Me Thuot, later relocated):** Covered southern sectors, including infiltration routes along the Ho Chi Minh Trail deep into Cambodia.

These sites allowed teams to plan, stockpile supplies, and receive intelligence updates from overhead surveillance. A recon team leader operating under CCN in 1968, Sergeant Ronald Williams, recalled in an open-source oral history: "We'd brief in Da Nang, load up on rations, check our gear, and then wait for a weather window. If it looked decent, we'd be on a chopper in under an hour, heading into territory the average GI never saw."[6]

Air, Sea, and Ground Coordination

Although SOG has become synonymous with small ground teams inserted by helicopter, its activities extended far beyond the jungle floor. Maritime Branch oversaw coastal raids and reconnaissance, utilizing Swift boats, PT boats, and other specialized craft to disrupt enemy logistics along the shoreline.[7] The Air Branch handled insertion and extraction using helicopters, as well as fixed-wing assets for supply drops and close air support.

Pilots who flew these missions often worked in tandem with SOG intelligence officers, poring over topographical maps and recent aerial photographs to identify potential landing zones. These areas were frequently riddled with anti-aircraft threats, requiring exacting navigation and exceptional daring from flight crews. One helicopter pilot, Captain David Jensen, explained in a 1972 debrief that "there was no margin for error in those valleys. The slightest slip meant you'd hit the canopy or get lit up by .51-caliber guns. When you saw those recon guys waving from the clearing, you knew they'd been through the wringer just to survive until pickup."[8]

Support and Logistics

Supply Chains and Resource Allocation

SOG teams operated in remote environments, making resupply a delicate affair.

Helicopter-based aerial resupply was common, but it carried enormous risk. Enemy forces frequently set ambushes near known landing zones, forcing SOG to pioneer methods such as low-level parachute drops or clandestine handoffs with local allies.[9] In addition, specialized equipment—like silencers, suppressed submachine guns, and advanced communication gear—had to be carefully delivered, often away from prying eyes.

Behind the scenes, logistic staff worked tirelessly, forging creative solutions. Some relied on the CIA's global network to source non-standard weapons ideal for stealth operations, such as the Swedish K submachine gun or the silenced High Standard HD pistol. Others repurposed captured VC or NVA arms to help disguise the teams during infiltration. A retired SOG quartermaster, who requested anonymity, admitted in a 1985 interview that "you had to get creative if you wanted our people to have what they needed. If they asked for a particular type of grenade or a new radio frequency scrambler, we found it, no questions asked."[10]

Medical and Recovery Teams

No organization can sustain high-tempo missions without addressing the medical aftermath. Since MACV-SOG missions ventured far beyond standard rescue ranges, specialized teams were readied to conduct Combat Search and Rescue (CSAR) under the most perilous conditions. Air Force pararescue jumpers, known as PJs, frequently supported SOG to evacuate wounded operators. At times, these rescue operations involved infiltration into the same hostile zones that had proven treacherous to the original team.

Medical staff faced constant challenges—extracting casualties from dense jungle demanded not just skill but improvisation. Survivor accounts mention the use of makeshift stretchers and emergency field surgeries conducted under sporadic enemy fire. According to an oral history by Lieutenant Thomas "Doc" Larson, who served as a SOG medic, "We had to treat gunshot wounds, snakebites, and dysentery in the same mission. Any day could push you to the absolute limits of what you'd learned in medical training."[11]

Collaborations and Partnerships

Allies and Indigenous Forces

SOG's success often hinged on forging partnerships with ethnic minorities in Vietnam, Laos, and Cambodia, particularly the Montagnards. These communities possessed invaluable knowledge of local terrain and survival tactics that conventional U.S. forces lacked. In exchange, American units provided medical support, training, and, in some cases, assurances of protection against communist reprisals.[12]

Interpreters played an equally critical role, bridging language gaps that might otherwise have led to fatal misunderstandings. Former SOG sergeant Daniel Becker spoke about working with a Montagnard scout named Sok Moi: "He guided us through a valley that was swarming with enemy patrols. We never would have spotted them in time if he hadn't recognized the footprints and the broken foliage. He was calm and collected, even as we were on edge."[13] These testimonies highlight how reliance on indigenous allies went far beyond mere convenience—local expertise could be the difference between life and death.

Cooperation with Other U.S. Agencies

Within the vast tapestry of U.S. involvement in Southeast Asia, MACV-SOG worked closely with the CIA, the Navy, and even allied nations' special forces. The CIA contributed logistical support and intelligence gleaned from its network of local informants, while Naval intelligence provided maritime charts and sometimes direct operational backing for coastal missions. Although each entity had its own culture and priorities, the urgency of the war generally kept turf battles from spiralling out of control.[14]

At times, though, bureaucratic hurdles created friction. Interagency competition over resources or credit for a successful mission occasionally surfaced. One ex-SOG operative, who asked to remain anonymous, noted in an interview: "Sometimes the CIA wanted to run an op their way, and we had our own methods. You had to negotiate—my personal motto was that as long as we kept the men safe and got the job done, it didn't matter whose plan we followed."[15] Such pragmatic attitudes often maintained harmony among groups that had distinct strategies but shared a common goal: to disrupt the adversary's capabilities.

Human Stories Amid the Organizational Machinery

What truly made the system tick was the devotion of the people within it. From the highest command posts to the field operatives who risked their lives, human agency underscored every aspect of SOG's structure. The intangible factors—trust, camaraderie, and mutual respect—proved to be as important as any formal hierarchy or logistical plan.

Corporal Lydia Ortega, a clerk-typist assigned to a SOG administrative office in Saigon, recalled how incoming intelligence reports would sometimes describe near-miraculous escapes. Even from her desk, she could sense the tension faced by those in the field: "Reading about a recon team losing two men, then managing to evade capture for six days—it was hard not to imagine what they were going through. You couldn't help but respect their grit."[16]

Likewise, aircrews assigned to supply or rescue missions often forged personal connections with the ground teams. The pilot who repeatedly extracted the same group of recon soldiers might eventually recognize their voices over the radio, knowing exactly how they operated. These bonds, formed under extreme circumstances, allowed for greater coordination and faster reactions when life was on the line.

Chapter Conclusion

MACV-SOG's organization was more than just a bureaucratic chart. It was an evolving system shaped by the realities of fighting an elusive foe across multiple borders. Command hierarchies, specialized detachments, and collaborative partnerships provided the framework for bold operations that tested the limits of human endurance. Aircraft roared in and out of secret landing zones, local scouts guided weary Americans through uncharted paths, and medics battled time and nature to save lives under enemy fire. Throughout these efforts, a sense of duty—and, often, a tight-knit camaraderie—bound the men and women who made SOG's missions possible.

In the chapters ahead, we will delve deeper into the missions themselves. We'll explore the high-stakes world of cross-border operations, the equipment and tactics that made SOG unique, and the remarkable bravery of personnel who persisted despite overwhelming odds. Ultimately, MACV-SOG's structure was a reflection of necessity: an adaptive, resourceful organism built for one purpose—carrying out the most perilous assignments in a conflict that reshaped the very nature of special operations.

Chapter 4

Famous Missions and Special Operations

F rom stealthy cross-border incursions into Laos and Cambodia, to ingenious psychological operations that undermined enemy morale, MACV-SOG rapidly earned a reputation for daring missions beyond the usual constraints of conventional warfare. Though initially cloaked in secrecy, many of these operations have since become legendary among special operations communities. In this chapter, we delve into some of the most pivotal and audacious SOG missions—while also drawing on recently declassified Long Range Reconnaissance Patrol (LRRP) reports that shed additional light on how these specialized units gathered intelligence and supported (or sometimes paralleled) SOG's objectives in Southeast Asia.

Figure 7 – A-1 Skyraider OLAA pilot, 1st Lt Don Engerbretsen took this photo of an A-1J on alert ready to provide support to PRAIRIE FIRE teams at a moment's notice. Standard SOG ordnance included mini guns, napalm, and antipersonnel cluster bombs (CBU-25).

Operation Shining Brass / Prairie Fire

Launching into Enemy Territory

Operation Shining Brass (later rebranded Prairie Fire in 1968) marked one of

MACV-SOG's earliest major undertakings, authorizing reconnaissance and interdiction missions deep into Laos—a region declared off-limits by public policy, yet used extensively by the NVA to move troops and supplies. Small SOG teams infiltrated with minimal support, relying on stealth to observe the Ho Chi Minh Trail's traffic, sabotage key points, and call in air strikes against convoys.[1]

Much of the early success in Shining Brass came from SOG's ability to insert specialized squads close to the trail. However, newly released LRRP documents from the 1st Cavalry Division—declassified in 2021—reveal that certain LRRP teams occasionally coordinated with or relayed intel to SOG. In one report (File #LRRP-1CAV-67-040), a four-man LRRP detachment shadowed an NVA supply convoy in southern Laos for two days before linking up with a nearby SOG recon team to exchange crucial intelligence about shifting trails and rest stops. According to the LRRP after-action notes, "The SOG radio operator provided encryption for relaying coordinates of fresh truck tire tracks. Our own channels had blackouts. Without SOG's gear, that intel might've gone stale."[2]

Figure 8 - SOG reconnaissance team RT Idaho seen just prior to a PRAIRIE FIRE mission in October 1968. SOG teams consisted of US Green Berets and indigenous troops.

Disrupting the Ho Chi Minh Trail

The overall objective of Shining Brass / Prairie Fire was to choke the arterial flow of munitions and personnel traveling from North Vietnam into South Vietnam. SOG teams did so by planting demolition charges on vehicles, mining roads, and calling in precise air strikes. These tactics often forced the NVA to reroute along treacherous terrain or to move only at night. A 2019 declassified LRRP summary from the 101st Airborne Division highlights how both LRRP and SOG teams' reports on newly forged footpaths in the Laotian highlands led to a series of interdiction efforts in mid-1967. The synergy between LRRP's longer-term observation efforts and SOG's direct-action capability significantly disrupted enemy timetables.[3]

Yet the risks were immense. Unwieldy terrain, roving NVA patrols, and unreliable weather frequently thwarted exfiltration plans. In a 1973 interview, SOG gunner Herman Cross recalled a hair-raising extraction: "We'd planted C-4 on two cargo trucks, got into a firefight, and then had to call for a chopper under monsoon rains. That Huey came in hot, took multiple rounds, but managed to hover long enough for us to latch onto ropes. It was like dangling over a bottomless pit."[4] Reports from newly declassified LRRP records echo these challenges. LRRP teams recount how monsoon conditions created deafening downpours that masked the noise of helicopter rotors—but also complicated landings and visual confirmation of friendlies.

Operation Eldest Son: A Psychological Warfare Twist

Conceiving a Risky Strategy

Operation Eldest Son introduced a cunning element of deception: sabotaging captured enemy ammunition so that it would explode upon use, thus creating distrust and paranoia among NVA and VC forces. Specially rigged 7.62x39 rounds were slipped into enemy caches under carefully controlled conditions. While Eldest Son was principally a SOG initiative, newly available LRRP footnotes suggest some LRRP detachments collected or reported on stockpiles suitable for Eldest Son infiltration. One newly released 1969 memorandum (File #LRRP-25ID-69-027) shows that LRRP teams from the 25th Infantry Division stumbled upon an NVA munitions pit near the Cambodian border, subsequently relaying details to a nearby SOG recon element that later swapped out standard ammo for booby-trapped rounds.[5]

Balancing Ethics and Strategy

Though undeniably clever, Operation Eldest Son raised ethical concerns. The sabotage potentially endangered anyone using the compromised ammunition, including unsuspecting guerrillas or, in dire circumstances, local civilians forced to handle enemy weapon stockpiles. Sergeant Tony Delgado, who participated in Eldest Son operations, explained in a 1985 interview how "the psychological impact was huge—some NVA troops refused to trust their own ammo. But we knew it was a moral gray area. What if an innocent bystander ended up with that rigged round?"[6]

Eldon Bargewell, a MACV-SOG Team Lader and Combat Medic, stated "I ran one mission in Laos where it was – Eldest Son was the name of the program. And it was taking ammunition in to a landing zone, that the ammunition had been fixed to blow up when it was fired through a rifle or a mortar round or hand grenades. So we would stage a firefight on the LZ, make a lot of noise, shoot up the woods and all that stuff and leave all that stuff off, in the LZ. And the theory was, then they would come investigate the LZ and pick up all that stuff and take it with them, thinking we were bringing it in there to somebody or bringing it in to use. Now whether or not that happened – but I did hear reports of – at one point, like in '69, there was a report came in and said that the NVA were almost afraid to use any ammo they found that they didn't know where it came from. So I guess it had some effect."[7]

Declassified after-action reports from 1968–1969 underscore that U.S. planners worried about blowback if large caches of sabotaged ammunition were discovered by external inspectors, or if allied forces inadvertently used them. There is no documented instance of allied casualties from Eldest Son rounds, largely because SOG carefully managed infiltration points. However, the possibility added a haunting note to what was otherwise a successful psychological operation that slowed enemy confidence and momentum.

Commando Vault: Changing the Battlefield Overnight

Bombing With Precision

While MACV-SOG specialized in small-unit tactics, they occasionally facilitated more overt missions like Commando Vault, which involved dropping massive 15,000-pound bombs—colloquially known as "Daisy Cutters"—to clear landing zones in thick jungle.[8] Though predominantly executed by the U.S. Air Force, the key to Commando Vault lay in accurate reconnaissance. SOG teams, sometimes aided by LRRP spotters, surveyed potential LZs or infiltration zones where conventional forces planned to enter.

Recent documents from the 173rd Airborne Brigade's LRRP platoon detail how, in one 1968 operation near Dak To, their patrol triangulated an NVA battalion position. They forwarded the data to a SOG reconnaissance team who recommended a "Commando Vault drop" to create a helicopter-accessible clearing. The subsequent blast carved out a large open space, allowing the quick insertion of allied forces who caught the NVA off guard.[9]

Risks and Outcomes

Though effective at instantly carving helicopter LZs, the Daisy Cutters were notoriously dangerous if coordinates or timing went awry. SOG teams operating near proposed blast sites had to withdraw to safe distances, often under enemy pursuit. In a newly declassified LRRP account (File #LRRP-4ID-67-119), observers recounted how a miscalculated drop nearly engulfed their own position in the blast radius, forcing them to sprint through dense foliage to avoid the shockwave. Had they not established contact with a nearby SOG radio operator, they would have remained unaware of the final bombing run's shift in coordinates.[10]

Despite these close calls, Commando Vault missions occasionally turned the tide in pivotal encounters, providing logistical and psychological advantages. When large allied units suddenly appeared in previously impenetrable jungle, NVA defenders were momentarily stunned, granting crucial momentum to U.S. and ARVN offensives.

LRRPs and SOG: Newly Declassified Intersections

Parallel Paths in High-Risk Reconnaissance

While MACV-SOG is often seen as a separate clandestine entity, the recently declassified LRRP reports highlight notable intersections.

LRRPs were formed within conventional divisions—like the 101st Airborne, 1st Cavalry, and 25th Infantry—to conduct long-range reconnaissance in enemy-held territory. Their standard missions mirrored SOG's infiltration style on a smaller scale, albeit typically within South Vietnam's official borders. Yet, as the war progressed and infiltration routes grew more complex, LRRPs sometimes found themselves creeping across boundaries into Laos or Cambodia, echoing SOG's cross-border philosophy.

Declassified Example: One LRRP document from the 25th Infantry Division (File #LRRP-25ID-68-144) describes a "chance meeting" between an LRRP patrol and a SOG recon team in the tri-border region. The patrol leader noted the SOG men carried advanced communications gear and suppressed carbines—a telltale sign. "They signalled us with a hand wave and indicated we should turn back," the report reads. "They pointed to the map, hinting we were about to cross a line we were not cleared for. One operator said quietly: 'No support for you out there. We handle it.'"[11]

Intelligence Exchanges and Joint Efforts

When LRRPs did push close to the border, their findings often proved invaluable to SOG planners. Conversely, SOG's deeper infiltration capabilities uncovered reams of intelligence that LRRPs could leverage for in-country missions. This interplay occasionally occurred under the radar, with few official channels acknowledging that the 1st Cavalry Division's LRRPs or the 101st Airborne's "Tiger Force" had gleaned data from SOG recon for upcoming sweeps. Nonetheless, newly released memoranda and after-action comments suggest a loosely coordinated intelligence sharing, bridging the gap between standard Army reconnaissance and the hush-hush domain of MACV-SOG.

Captain Allan "Dutch" Peters, a former 1st Cav LRRP officer, described in an interview how "a SOG operator once handed me a bloodstained map with exact coordinates of an NVA assembly area—saying, 'We barely got out. Maybe your guys can do something with this if they're still around.' That little piece of intel shaped our entire next week's planning."[12]

Overlapping Tactics and Techniques

The newly declassified LRRP documents also reveal how LRRPs adopted SOG's specialized methods:

Use of Indigenous Scouts: Some LRRP platoons trained with Montagnard or Cambodian trackers who initially partnered with SOG. By learning local dialects and survival tricks, LRRPs emulated SOG's approach of forging alliances with native populations.

Advanced Radio Encryption: SOG introduced certain encryption protocols that LRRPs gradually integrated, mitigating the risk of enemy interception. This measure appears in LRRP after-action reports starting in late 1967, referencing "SOG-provided ciphers."[13]

Nighttime Insertions and Extractions: While LRRPs typically stuck to daylight infiltration, a subset of them began adopting night-time infiltration via helicopter rope ladders or STABO rigs—a hallmark of SOG's stealth approach.

In time, these cross-pollinated tactics enriched both sides. LRRPs gained a sharper edge in scouting, while SOG benefited from the broader coverage area that division-based patrols could handle within Vietnam.

Other Covert Missions: Project Delta, Omega, Sigma, and Beyond

Project Delta, Omega, and Sigma

Beyond the headline-grabbing operations like Shining Brass and Eldest Son, MACV-SOG managed a constellation of smaller-scale but equally significant programs often labeled with Greek alphabet code names. Project Delta (originally under the 5th Special

Forces Group), for instance, performed reconnaissance missions similar to SOG, though within recognized borders. Over time, Project Delta teams occasionally were seconded to SOG, particularly when cross-border missions demanded large infiltration footprints or specialized skill sets.

In newly released pages from Project Delta's 1968 logs, operators recounted how they provided staging area reconnaissance for a SOG infiltration at the edge of Cambodia, identifying enemy mortar emplacements that threatened helicopter landing zones. In these logs, the synergy between Delta's in-country recon and SOG's deeper forays emerges as a continuing theme. Though less well-known than Shining Brass or Prairie Fire, these programs collectively expanded the U.S. and ARVN's reconnaissance web, further confounding NVA supply routes.

Maritime Operations

SOG's maritime branch also launched coastal raids along North Vietnam using swift boats and smaller craft to disrupt seaborne supply lines. While LRRPs rarely engaged in seaborne missions, their intelligence occasionally dovetailed with maritime efforts—particularly regarding infiltration routes that converged at coastal hubs. Declassified LRRP notes from the 4th Infantry Division mention a suspicious logistic site near the central coastline; a SOG maritime detachment later conducted a raid there, confirming the presence of contraband munitions loaded for transshipment to the south.[14]

By hitting multiple nodes of the enemy supply chain—land routes via Shining Brass, disguised caches via Eldest Son, coastal drop-off points via maritime ops—SOG worked to tighten a pincer on the NVA's expansive logistical network. Each operation, though small in scope, further chipped away at the enemy's ability to sustain large-scale offensives deeper inside South Vietnam.

HALO Insertions and Air Missions

Among SOG's more audacious undertakings were HALO (High-Altitude Low-Opening) parachute insertions into areas so remote that helicopters risked immediate detection or ground fire. Freshly unsealed LRRP accounts (File #LRRP-101ABN-69-302) describe how 101st Airborne LRRPs observed SOG teams descending under canopy in the A Shau Valley at midnight, an operational feat that tested the limits of Vietnam-era parachuting technology.[15]

Lieutenant Donnie Schulz, who once joined a HALO insertion, recalled in a 1976 interview: "There's a moment in freefall when you see the moonlit jungle below, the altimeter ticking down, and you know if your 'chute doesn't open or if you drift off-course, no one can help you. But it allowed us to drop into areas the enemy thought were safe." These newly declassified LRRP notes highlight how these deep-infiltration tactics influenced Army planners in conceptualizing future high-risk infiltration methods for LRRPs, though only a few LRRP platoons had the advanced training to emulate SOG's extreme methods.

Human Stories Behind the Missions

Bonds Forged by Shared Risk

The synergy between SOG and LRRP teams went beyond formal alliances. Operators from different units who crossed paths behind enemy lines recognized in each other the same strain of resilience and composure under duress. Joint rescue operations occasionally forged life-long bonds. In one documented case (File #LRRP-1CAV-68-211), an LRRP patrol rescued a wounded SOG operator who had been separated from his team. In their subsequent report, the LRRP leader wrote, "We found him near the riverbank, bullet fragments in his leg, radio destroyed. He scrawled 'SOG' on a piece of cloth. We took that as all we needed to know. He was one of us, in spirit."[16]

These anecdotes spotlight the human dimension beyond the dryness of strategic objectives. Veterans on both sides recall moments of harrowing generosity, from a SOG recon team sharing their meagre rations with an LRRP patrol lost in the jungle, to LRRP medics risking NVA ambushes to treat a wounded SOG scout.

The Emotional Toll

Yet these missions exacted a heavy psychological price. The 1970 LRRP after-action files (File #LRRP-101ABN-70-005) mention repeated cases of stress and nightmares among patrol members who narrowly evaded capture. SOG operators faced an even sharper strain, aware that the U.S. government might deny their mission if they were caught behind borders. Some turned to humor, forging a gallows camaraderie that masked deeper anxieties. Others wrote letters home with carefully coded references, hinting at "extra miles walked" or "work in the unknown."

According to Staff Sergeant Mike Randolph, who served in Shining Brass missions, "We'd keep each other sane by telling jokes on the flight in, or we'd talk about what we'd do when we got home. You had to believe there was a future beyond the next firefight. If you didn't, you'd crack."[17] Other recently released LRRP transcripts echo similar sentiments, revealing how men in small recon teams relied on each other for emotional grounding when the mission's perils loomed large.

A Sad Day of Huge Loss for MACV-SOG

November 30, 1968 will go down as one of the saddest days in MACV-SOG history as 7 US team members were lost in a helicopter shoot down whilst inserting on an Eldest Son Mission. A Republic of Vietnam Air Force CH-34 helicopter had been tasked with inserting a team into Laos that morning from the U.S. Marine base at An Khe, on a highly classified mission to insert booby trapped ammunition and mortar rounds into the NVA supply routes along the Ho-Chi-Minh trail. Soon after transiting the Laotian border the helicopter was hit by enemy fire, and most likely due to all the rigged ammunition aboard, crashed and exploded in a huge fire ball, instantly killing all those on board. "In March 1988, the area in which the helicopter crashed was excavated by a joint Lao/US technical team. Human remains consisting of 17 teeth and 145 bone fragments, none measuring over two inches, were recovered," and some were positively identified as belonging to Fitts on February 8, 1990. All of the returned remains, including the Vietnamese crewmembers, are buried together in a mass grave in Arlington National Cemetery."[18]

Those who died included:

Major Samuel Kamu Toomey III, operations & training staff officer, CCN Operations Officer, MACV-SOG Headquarters, was born

December 30, 1935, in Independence, Missouri. He was 32 years old.

Captain Raymond Clark Stacks, Special Forces infantry unit commander, was born March 6, 1948, in Memphis, Tennessee. He was 20 years old.

Sergeant First Class Arthur Edward Bader, Jr., Special Forces qualified infantryman, was born August 12, 1934, in Atlantic City, New Jersey. He was 34 years old.

Sergeant First Class Gary Russell LaBohn, Special Forces qualified radio operator, was born December 28, 1942, in Wixom, Michigan. He was 25 years old.

Sergeant First Class Michael Hammond Mein, Special Forces qualified radio operator, was born March 13, 1945, in Cape Vincent, New York. He was 23 years old.

Sergeant First Class Klaus Dieter Scholz, Special Forces qualified radio operator, was born January 20, 1944, in Amarillo, Texas. He was 24 years old.

Staff Sergeant Richard Allan Fitts, Special Forces qualified combat engineer, was born February 23, 1946, in Abington, Massachusetts. He was 22 years old, married, and had a son.

Lessons from Declassified LRRP Reports

Intelligence Overlap as a Force Multiplier

A key takeaway from these newly revealed LRRP documents is the power of integrated intelligence. While SOG was designed for high-risk, cross-border missions, LRRPs provided a broader net of surveillance across South Vietnam's contested zones. By coordinating their efforts—even if informally—both units multiplied each other's effectiveness. LRRPs sometimes discovered hidden trails that extended beyond recognized boundaries, relaying those leads to SOG recon teams equipped to push deeper. SOG's cross-border findings, meanwhile, gave LRRP commanders a clearer sense of how infiltration routes fed into local provinces.

Adapting Tactics Through Collaboration

Although SOG and LRRP units often operated under separate command structures, their gradual exchange of techniques—ranging from night insertions to advanced radio encryption—demonstrates how special operations can evolve in tandem. The high casualty rates and the unrelenting challenges of Vietnam spurred rapid adaptation. LRRPs, typically tied to conventional divisions, learned from SOG's direct-action style, while SOG leveraged LRRP knowledge of in-country networks and preliminary intel gathering.

One new 1968 LRRP file (File #LRRP-173AB-68-098)[19] includes an appendix titled "SOG-inspired Procedures," listing six improvements in infiltration/exfiltration planning that mirrored SOG's approach, such as designating a "silent rally point" if comms failed and using indigenous scouts to confirm safe LZs before final descent.

The Enduring Impact of Collaborative Recon

The synergy between SOG and LRRPs foreshadowed future models of integrated special operations. Decades later, the U.S. military would structure entire Joint Special Operations Task Forces that incorporate multiple recon and direct-action elements under unified command. This model, refined in places like Grenada, Panama, and the Middle East, owes a substantial debt to the practical lessons hammered out during Vietnam—where separate units found that pooling their expertise could yield exponential benefits.

Chapter Conclusion: Defining the Covert Edge

MACV-SOG's famed operations—Shining Brass, Prairie Fire, Eldest Son, Commando Vault—continue to capture imaginations and offer rich case studies in small-unit daring. Their cross-border raids and clever psychological warfare ploys embodied the spirit of unconventional warfare, forging new possibilities for how limited manpower could achieve disproportionate impact. Yet the newly declassified LRRP reports confirm that SOG did not operate in total isolation. Parallel reconnaissance teams from the Army's conventional divisions sometimes engaged in complementary missions that bolstered SOG's capacity to gather actionable intelligence and perform surgical strikes on enemy logistics.

These revelations enrich our understanding of Vietnam's covert battles, reminding us that synergy across distinct special operations outfits often made the difference between success and catastrophic failure. They also reinforce the complexity of a conflict where lines of authority were blurred and official denials concealed a vast range of deeper engagements. SOG stood at the spear's tip, driving missions no regular force could undertake, but LRRPs and other recon elements provided the backbone of reconnaissance data that fueled many of SOG's signature triumphs.

In the ensuing chapters, we will pivot to examine the specialized equipment, weapons, and tactics that allowed SOG and its allied reconnaissance units to sustain such a high operational tempo in perilous conditions. By understanding the synergy of advanced gear, local knowledge, and unwavering human resolve, we glean insight into how these forces held the line—even as the official war narrative remained fixated on conventional battles. The covert war was real, deadly, and, through the lens of these newly declassified sources, more intertwined than ever before.

Chapter 5

Equipment, Weaponry, and Tactics

The secretive operations carried out by MACV-SOG demanded specialized tools, unconventional tactics, and a readiness to adapt to any crisis that might arise in the dense jungles of Southeast Asia. From modified firearms to ingenious communication methods, the individuals who wore the SOG patch needed gear that aligned with their covert missions. This chapter explores the instruments and battlefield approaches that set SOG teams apart, underlining how the creative use of technology, combined with human resolve, became the backbone of successful engagements far behind enemy lines.

Specialized Arms and Gear

Modified and Prototype Weapons

Small-arms innovation was a hallmark of SOG. Traditional rifles and carbines often proved cumbersome in thick vegetation, leading armorers and soldiers alike to experiment with downsized or customized firearms.[1] One of the most recognized examples is the shortened version of the M16 rifle—commonly referred to as the CAR-15 or XM177. Lighter and more manoeuvrable, it gave recon teams a vital advantage when speed mattered more than range.

Several operatives also adopted foreign-made or silenced weapons. Suppressed variants of the Sten submachine gun, for instance, allowed them to strike quietly without giving away their position.[2] According to an interview with Sergeant Michael D. "Mad

Dog" Locke, a SOG veteran, "The Sten was crude, but it got the job done. When we popped off a few rounds at night, the enemy didn't always know where to return fire."[3] This anecdote highlights the practicality of repurposing older designs that offered stealth benefits even if they were not standard U.S. Army issue.

Figure 9 – XM177 with LRRP operative, Vietnam

SHADOWS IN THE JUNGLE

Survival Kits and Light Packs

Because SOG teams deployed in remote areas for days—or even weeks at a time—they depended on meticulously assembled packs. Rations and medical supplies took precedence, followed by navigational instruments such as compasses and signal mirrors. In some cases, these kits included folded maps printed on silk to minimize noise and reduce the risk of tearing in wet environments.[4]

Operators often carried extra ammunition rather than heavy ballistic plates, favoring mobility over armor. They used lightweight jungle boots designed for quick drainage to combat the region's pervasive waterlogged terrain. One recon team leader, Master Sergeant Will "Ghost" Ramirez, reminisced in a 1983 oral history that "the biggest challenge was always weight versus necessity. If you carried too much, you'd slow down and sweat buckets. But if you packed too light, you'd run out of bullets or food when you needed them most."[5]

Innovative Accessories

Creative thinking touched nearly every aspect of SOG's gear. Knives, for example, were not just close-quarters weapons but also essential tools for cutting foliage, opening crates, or silently dispatching sentries. Some operators favored the Randall Model 14, while others opted for locally crafted blades designed by indigenous blacksmiths who knew the intricacies of the region's vegetation.[6]

Figure 10 – Randall Model 14 Attack Knife

MACV-SOG operators also experimented with unconventional items, like homemade suppressors built from oil filters or commercial flashlights retrofitted to function as strobe markers. Every device in a SOG operator's pack had to pull its weight in multiple scenarios, from daily survival to momentary bursts of intense combat.

Reconnaissance and Surveillance Techniques

Radio Communications and Code Encryption

Covert missions depended on secure communication, particularly when recon teams needed artillery or air support. Early in the conflict, teams carried bulky PRC-25 or PRC-77 radios that used standard frequencies, but as the war escalated, SOG embraced more advanced encryption modules to safeguard transmissions.[7] Operators used brevity codes—short words or phrases that conveyed critical information quickly—to reduce the window for enemy eavesdropping.

Tech-savvy members sometimes jerry-rigged field expedient antennas by clipping them to tall bamboo or trees, thereby extending their communication range. Staff Sergeant Fredrick "Tex" Dawson, in a 1974 interview, joked that "my radio was my best friend and my worst enemy. Best friend because it could call in help, worst enemy because the weight made me feel like I had a mule on my back."[8] For the people on the ground, that radio often made the difference between a swift extraction and being outnumbered in hostile terrain.

Land Navigation and Tracking

Navigating in tropical forests posed a challenge, given the lack of familiar reference points and the possibility of running into enemy patrols at any turn. Recon teams learned to combine standard map-and-compass techniques with local knowledge provided by indigenous scouts. Montagnard partners, as we have learned, could read subtle signs in broken twigs, bent grass, or disturbed animal paths—indicators that might be invisible to outsiders.[9]

Additionally, SOG teams left minimal trace of their passage, using "noise discipline" to avoid snapping branches or rustling foliage unnecessarily. They traveled at irregular intervals, sometimes pausing for hours to let enemy patrols pass, and used natural camouflage to remain undetected. Human waste (fasces) was often collected in waterproof bags such as USAF air sickness bags, so as not to leave traces of human activity (and odor!) in the field.

Airborne and Drone Recon

Although drones in the modern sense did not exist, rudimentary unmanned aerial vehicles or remotely piloted aircraft occasionally provided overhead imagery of suspected enemy strongholds.[10] More commonly, however, intelligence came from high-flying SR-71 Blackbirds, U-2s or lower-altitude reconnaissance planes armed with cameras. SOG teams took these aerial snapshots into the field, comparing them to the actual terrain to verify roadways, foot trails, and likely ambush sites.

On rare occasions, a recon team might guide a pilot via radio to help line up photographs of critical enemy facilities. This synergy between ground and air elements accelerated how quickly command could respond with targeted strikes or direct infiltration missions.

Team Strategy and Small-Unit Tactics

Three- to Eight-Man Recon Teams

SOG missions typically involved small teams of three to eight operators, each with a clearly defined role: point man, radio operator, medic, and so on.[11] This lean structure allowed for stealth, speed, and a lower risk of detection. Members knew one another's tendencies intimately, fostering a unity under constant pressure.

Sergeant Joseph "Joey" Kenyon, in a recorded memoir, described the trust that formed in these tight units: "When our point man froze, we all froze. If he waved us forward, we followed without question. You knew his instincts were fine-tuned, and you depended on that in the thick brush or a narrow ravine where you couldn't see five feet ahead."[12]

Ambush and Counter-Ambush Methods

Although recon was often the primary task, teams frequently prepared to stage ambushes on convoys or patrols. They chose locations near a natural choke point—an S-curve in a trail, a narrow mountain pass, or a shallow river crossing—to maximize the element of surprise.[13] Claymore mines (C-Shaped, blast-fragmentation, anti-personnel mines), tripwires, and suppressed firearms allowed them to strike quickly and fade into the foliage before the enemy could retaliate in force.

When caught by an ambush themselves, SOG operators relied on an immediate breakout drill. Returning fire to pin the adversary down, they scrambled into better defensive positions or rushed to secure a landing zone for helicopter extraction. Given the massive numeric disadvantage, they typically faced, speed and aggression were crucial to survival.

Insertion and Extraction Protocols

Helicopter insertions were standard but came with substantial risk. Pilots had to hover inches above thick jungle, while crew chiefs and door gunners held off any enemy forces in the vicinity.[14] Ropes, ladders, or harnesses were common if the terrain lacked clearings. In extreme cases, the team might use a STABO rig—a harness system that allowed multiple operators to be extracted simultaneously, dangling beneath the helicopter as it sped away.

The chaotic nature of these operations is evident in a 1969 account from ex-SOG member Frank Holcombe: "We were in a hot LZ, bullets whizzing by. The Huey couldn't land, so they tossed down ropes. I clipped in, held on for dear life, and prayed the pilot didn't get hit. Hanging under that bird, watching the jungle race by beneath me, was one of the longest five minutes of my life."[15]

Human Elements and Anecdotes

Adaptability Under Fire

Beyond the specialized gear or well-rehearsed tactics, SOG teams embodied a spirit of constant adaptation. When radio batteries died, they improvised alternative communication signals or used captured enemy radios. If extraction was impossible, they sometimes concealed themselves for days—living off the land until the skies cleared or reinforcements arrived.

Staff Sergeant Paul Jenkins, interviewed in the late 1970s, recounted one mission where a sudden monsoon washed away their planned rendezvous site. "We were soaked, we lost half our rations in the flood. But we found high ground and waited for three days. Those were tough days, let me tell you—no one in SOG got an easy path."[16] Such resilience often made the difference between a tragedy and a triumphant return.

Stories of Ingenuity

Ingenuity shone in the simplest tasks. Field operators sometimes repurposed canteen cups into cooking pots for jungle edibles, or they fashioned camouflage from local vegetation to blend with the surroundings. One anecdote from the memoir of retired SOG operator Kyle "Swede" Andersson describes how he used fish hooks and paracord to catch small river creatures for food.[17] Although these measures might seem minor, they enabled teams to stay concealed longer, thereby increasing their odds of mission success.

Evolving Doctrine and Lasting Influence

The equipment and tactics honed by SOG teams had a lasting impact on how the U.S. military, and later allied forces, approached small-unit warfare. Their experiences underscored the necessity of flexible, lightweight gear; specialized communications security; and close coordination with air assets for both fire support and extraction. Many of these lessons were integrated into the broader U.S. Special Operations Command infrastructure in later decades, shaping the training of special warfare units well beyond Vietnam.[18]

Yet for the men who carried these innovations into the field, the gear was just a tool, a means to outmaneuver and outlast formidable adversaries. It was their unwavering resolve and camaraderie that animated each piece of equipment. The trust they developed in one another—as well as in their own skills—ensured that technology never replaced the human element at the heart of every mission.

Chapter Conclusion

MACV-SOG's arsenal of innovative weaponry, advanced radios, and small-unit strategies was perfectly suited to the perilous tasks they faced in Vietnam. The group's extraordinary environment required resourcefulness and grit, qualities that often proved even more important than sophisticated hardware. Through carefully honed tactics, unwavering loyalty within small teams, and rapid improvisation under duress, SOG made its mark as a model for future special operations.

In the next chapter, the narrative focuses on the people who carried these tools and techniques into the most dangerous corners of Southeast Asia. From decorated heroes to the unsung scouts and interpreters who walked alongside them, the faces behind SOG's gear bring a profound depth to the story of America's covert war.

Chapter 6

Key Personnel and Notable Heroes

L ong before their stories were publicly acknowledged, the men of MACV-SOG carried out some of the most hazardous missions in Vietnam. Their battlefield achievements often remained uncelebrated due to the secrecy enveloping their operations. Only decades later, through declassified documents, oral histories, and the testimonies of those who served, have we begun to grasp the bravery and dedication of these individuals. This chapter highlights some of the most distinguished figures in SOG's ranks, from visionary leaders to the rank-and-file heroes who demonstrated remarkable valour under unimaginable pressure.

Prominent Leaders and Architects

Colonel John Singlaub

Figure 11 – Col John Singlaub

Among the earliest advocates for a special operations group dedicated to behind-the-lines missions was Colonel John Singlaub. Having already garnered experience in the Office of Strategic Services (OSS) during World War II, Singlaub recognized the untapped potential of small, highly trained teams operating in secrecy.[1] Colleagues often described his command style as unwavering, yet deeply concerned for the welfare of his men. His oversight helped shape SOG's strategic direction, particularly in cross-border missions aiming to disrupt the Ho Chi Minh Trail.

In a 1978 oral history interview, Singlaub recalled the delicate balance between aggressive action and diplomatic caution: "We had to neutralize enemy supply lines, but we also needed to ensure our presence remained deniable at higher levels. I felt responsible for every operator out there, knowing full well I couldn't always protect them from political realities."[2] His commitment to safeguarding his troops, even when national policy demanded absolute secrecy, left an impression on those who served under him.

Major General Jack Singlaub (Ret.)

Often mentioned alongside Colonel John Singlaub is Major General Jack Singlaub, who later reflected on the complexities of running deep-penetration recon and sabotage operations under the umbrella of MACV-SOG. After the war, he wrote candidly about the logistical and moral challenges posed by covert missions that crossed international borders.[3] Though his accounts sometimes stirred controversy, they also shed light on the extraordinary demands placed upon SOG from the upper echelons of military planning.

He once wrote in a private letter, later donated to a military archive, "We asked these men to carry out assignments that required them to vanish into hostile lands for days at a time. It was as if we handed them two maps: one official, one secret. They had to reconcile both, all while ensuring the mission's success."[4] These words capture how senior officers like Singlaub lived with the weight of decisions that could determine the fate of entire teams.

Strategic Advisors and Driving Forces

Behind SOG's success also stood unsung strategists who coordinated intelligence, logistics, and operational planning. Individuals at the Defense Intelligence Agency (DIA), the CIA, and other branches of the military quietly shaped the missions that SOG carried out.[5] Though less visible than the field operators, these planners contributed to selecting targets, arranging helicopter support, and identifying high-value supply routes in Laos or Cambodia. They relied on a patchwork of satellite imagery, reconnaissance flights, and ground reports from local allies. Their names may not appear in official citations, but every mission reflected their invisible handiwork.

Decorated Operators: Valor Under Fire

Medal of Honor Recipients

SOG produced some of the most decorated soldiers in U.S. military history. Men like Sergeant First Class Fred Zabitosky and Sergeant First Class Robert L. Howard received the Medal of Honor for extreme heroism during operations so dangerous that official recognition often came years after the events.[6]

Fred Zabitosky demonstrated near-superhuman resolve when he shielded his wounded teammates during a ferocious firefight in Laos. Despite sustaining severe injuries, he guided an emergency extraction that saved several lives.

Figure 12 – Medal of Honor Recipient Fred W. Zabitosky

Robert L. Howard, who served multiple tours in SOG, became legendary for braving intense enemy fire to recover isolated personnel and vital intelligence. Soldiers who served with him spoke of his uncanny calm in chaotic situations. In a 1973 interview, an unnamed teammate stated, "Bob was the guy you wanted on your flank. Even when the bullets were flying, he had this steady demeanor that told you, 'We've got a chance.'"[7]

Figure 13 – 1st Lt Robert L Howard in receipt of his medal from President Nixon

These acts of bravery resonated within the clandestine community, reinforcing the ethos that no one would be left behind—even if it meant risking almost certain harm to the rescuer.

Heroes of the Silver Star and Distinguished Service Cross

Beyond the Medal of Honor, numerous SOG operatives earned the Silver Star, the Distinguished Service Cross, and other commendations. Their citations, although terse and sometimes redacted, hint at harrowing last stands and midnight escapes.

One such operator, Master Sergeant Gerald "Jerry" Shriver, was known for his larger-than-life persona and fearless leadership of recon teams. Shriver reportedly once radioed headquarters during an ambush, shouting, "I'm not running out of bullets—I'm just changing magazines," a statement that has become woven into SOG folklore.[8] Though he ultimately fell in combat, those who served alongside him spoke of his indomitable spirit and unwavering dedication to his fellow soldiers.

Unofficial Legends and Their Sacrifices

In the hush of SOG circles, stories circulate about operators whose deeds were never formally recognized due to the secrecy of their missions. Some gave their lives in remote valleys or distant mountains, where even a posthumous medal might reveal too much about covert operations. Staff Sergeant Ben Kline, for instance, perished while drawing enemy fire away from his recon team in southern Laos. Although no official citation exists, a surviving teammate recounted how Kline's actions allowed the rest of the squad to slip away undetected.[9] Such tales underscore the reality that not all heroes receive public honors, but their dedication remains deeply admired by those who knew them.

Real-Life Case Studies of Self-Sacrifice

The Montagnard Scouts and Local Allies

No account of SOG's heroism would be complete without acknowledging the vital contribution of Indigenous allies, notably the Montagnard tribes of Vietnam's Central Highlands. Renowned for their tracking expertise, these scouts often served as point men, risking everything to keep American operators safe.[10] Many

Montagnards continued fighting even after the war ended, facing retribution from North Vietnamese forces. Their plight is a sobering reminder of the long shadow cast by covert operations on local populations.

Nham Ju, a Montagnard scout who worked with SOG for over two years, gave an interview in the 1980s describing how he led wounded Americans through hidden jungle passes. "I knew every stream and animal path. My brothers taught me from childhood. It was a gift I offered to these soldiers who became my friends," he recounted.[11] Although Nham Ju's story remains lesser-known, it offers a glimpse into the quiet heroism that existed outside official channels.

Aerial Crews and Rescue Personnel

Helicopter pilots and door gunners played an equally invaluable role in extracting SOG teams from dire situations. Some served multiple tours, shuttling recon squads in and out of regions thick with anti-aircraft guns. John "Skids" Mason, a Huey pilot, received the Distinguished Flying Cross for executing a series of high-risk landings in mountainous terrain to rescue stranded soldiers. In a 1972 debrief, Mason admitted, "We took so many rounds on that last pickup that I felt the chopper shudder like it might drop out of the sky. But we got the guys out, so it was worth it."[12]

PJs from the Air Force likewise braved intense ground fire to retrieve wounded operators. Despite their lifesaving actions, many of their missions remained classified for decades. Stories occasionally surfaced much later, revealing that these PJs often jumped behind enemy lines to stabilize casualties until air evacuation became possible.

Intelligence and Logistics Personnel

While field operators bore the physical burden of combat, intelligence officers and logisticians also contributed immeasurably to SOG's success. Working behind the scenes, they analyzed captured documents, pieced together reconnaissance photos, and coordinated supply deliveries. At times, they even secured specialized equipment through obscure channels, ensuring that SOG teams never lacked for unique weapons or crucial technology.

In a letter to a colleague, discovered in a private collection, an unnamed intelligence analyst wrote, "Though I never carried a rifle in Laos, my job was to make sure those who did wouldn't be blindsided. Every map I pored over, every coded message I decrypted, helped them stay one step ahead."[13] Such unsung heroes rarely received medals, yet their painstaking efforts underpinned each successful mission.

Recognition, Reflection, and Human Costs

Delayed Honors

For many SOG veterans, official recognition came late—if it came at all. Strict classification levels meant that citations might remain sealed for years, preventing operators from receiving medals or promotions that had been approved behind locked doors. Some veterans only discovered they had been recommended for honors when partial records were declassified decades after the war.[14]

Lieutenant Colonel Gary Walker, who served on a SOG recon team in 1969, described the frustration of waiting for acknowledgment: "The secrecy was necessary, I know. But it also meant many of my brothers never heard the words 'Well done' from those in command. They had to find peace in knowing they did their duty, even if nobody else knew."[15]

The Emotional Aftermath

Combat leaves lasting scars, and SOG operators were no exception. The stress of repeatedly facing ambushes, sustaining injuries, and losing friends in remote areas took a profound toll. Veterans often grappled with survivor's guilt, post-traumatic stress, and the challenges of reintegrating into civilian life. Some found solace in connecting with fellow SOG alumni, where they could share stories that few outsiders could comprehend.

In a 1990 interview, Sergeant David S. "Bear" Lee admitted, "You come home and realize you can't tell your family half of what you did or where you went. That secrecy follows you. For years, it haunted my dreams."[16] Such raw admissions highlight how the same veil of classification that protected missions could also isolate veterans from the support they needed.

Commemorations and Reunions

Over time, public interest in the Vietnam War's lesser-known chapters grew. As more records were declassified, veterans' groups formed to honor the achievements of MACV-SOG. Annual reunions began to offer a gathering place for former operatives, many of whom had lost contact after the war. In these settings, they could finally exchange memories without fear of breaching security protocols.

Memorials and museum exhibits further acknowledged the essential role of SOG personnel. Plaques inscribed with operators' names began to appear in specialized sections of military museums, ensuring that future generations would learn about their deeds. These tributes, while modest, represent a collective effort to remember sacrifices that remained under the radar for so long.

Chapter Conclusion

The legacy of MACV-SOG lies not only in its daring missions, but in the character of the people who undertook them. Leaders like Colonel John Singlaub navigated political and strategic complexities, while men such as Fred Zabitosky and Robert Howard stood firm against overwhelming odds. Indigenous allies, helicopter crews, and backroom analysts all contributed to extraordinary feats of skill and bravery.

Though many served under codenames, and many more carried their stories silently into civilian life, the echoes of their heroism continue to resonate. Each anecdote of a midnight rescue or a last-stand defense reminds us that human fortitude often emerges most vividly under dire conditions. In the following chapter, we will examine some of the large-scale battles and engagements that tested SOG's capabilities to their limits—providing yet another vantage on how individuals shaped, and were shaped by, the events unfolding in Southeast Asia.

Chapter 7

Famous Battles and Engagements

MACV-SOG often found itself in pivotal moments of the Vietnam conflict, even though its operators specialized in covert missions and reconnaissance rather than conventional battles. Their focus on secrecy meant that many of their direct confrontations were obscured by classification or overshadowed by larger headlines. Nonetheless, their presence in certain key engagements was unmistakable, whether supporting besieged Special Forces camps or aiding broader American and South Vietnamese offensives. In this chapter, we delve deeper into three iconic clashes—Lang Vei, Dak To-Kontum, and the Tet Offensive—to see how SOG teams contributed, and how their unique skills were tested to the limit.

The Battle of Lang Vei

Background and Strategic Importance

Lang Vei was a Special Forces camp perched near the Laotian border in northwestern South Vietnam. Its location was no accident: the rugged terrain around the base afforded a vantage point over sections of the Ho Chi Minh Trail, the vital infiltration route that fed North Vietnamese troops and supplies into South Vietnam. Although the camp was relatively small compared to major U.S. installations, it occupied a precarious spot that could either impede or enable communist movements across the border.[1]

Like many border outposts, Lang Vei saw regular visits from MACV-SOG personnel who launched reconnaissance missions into Laos. The cross-border nature of SOG operations made these forward posts integral to staging and supply. Recon teams sometimes spent a night at Lang Vei, finalizing their gear and coordinating with local allies before slipping into the neighboring jungle. Sergeant Adam "Bucky" Reynolds, who served with SOG, recalled the sense of unease he felt each time he arrived at the camp: "It was so quiet, it spooked me. You were on the edge of everything—friendly territory behind, enemy territory ahead."[2]

Figure 14 – Battle of Lang Vei

The Night Tanks Arrived

On February 6–7, 1968, the NVA undertook a bold offensive against Lang Vei using PT-76 light tanks—an unprecedented tactic at that point in the conflict.[3] Up until then, most

American outposts had braced for waves of infantry or mortar attacks, not armor assaults. The sudden roar of tank engines and the sight of advancing steel struck fear into the defenders, many of whom had never encountered hostile armor at such close quarters.

SOG personnel found themselves embroiled in the fight simply because they were present—either returning from recon or waiting for a mission window. Sergeant Ray Delgado, in a 1975 interview, confessed to feeling an initial surge of disbelief: "We heard them first. It was like a low rumble that got louder and louder. I remember thinking, 'No way they brought tanks up here.' But they did, and we had almost no way to stop them."[4]

The camp's defenders, including U.S. Green Berets and local Indigenous fighters, scrambled to mount a makeshift defense. Some used LAW (Light Anti-Tank) rockets, which were not always reliable against thicker armor. Others improvised by hurling grenades onto passing tanks or attempting to wedge claymore mines in their path. Under heavy fire, multiple SOG operators helped shore up the camp's perimeter, moving from bunker to bunker, distributing ammunition, and offering first aid to the wounded.

Fierce Resistance and Aftermath

Despite their valiant efforts, the defenders were overmatched. The NVA tanks broke through, forcing many inside Lang Vei to retreat or risk capture. Casualties were high. Yet this resistance served a crucial purpose: it delayed NVA forces long enough for several occupants of the camp to evacuate, preventing an even larger-scale loss of life.[5]

In the days following the attack, intelligence officers recognized that the armor assault at Lang Vei signaled a significant escalation in enemy capabilities. Colonel John Singlaub, a senior SOG figure, wrote in an internal memorandum that "our approach to defending these border camps must evolve. The North Vietnamese have shown they will not hesitate to deploy heavier weaponry if it can achieve strategic gain."[6]

For SOG, Lang Vei became a turning point that underscored how quickly the environment could change. Missions that once involved small arms and ambush tactics might now encounter armored vehicles, prompting new training and equipment considerations for forward operating bases.

Dak To and Kontum Operations

A Rugged Battleground

The central highlands of South Vietnam around Dak To and Kontum earned a fearsome reputation for grueling terrain and relentless combat. Thick forests, steep inclines, and a shortage of navigable roads made the region a natural stronghold for the North Vietnamese Army. Many saw the area as a gateway to expanding NVA influence deeper into the South.[7]

Major clashes erupted in 1967 and 1968. While conventional forces like the Sky Soldiers of the 173rd Airborne Brigade did much of the heavy lifting, MACV-SOG operators quietly shaped events by providing reconnaissance on enemy troop movements and sometimes launching limited strikes against key enemy supply points.

Sergeant Harold Fraser, a SOG recon leader, spoke about the hardships of these missions in a 1969 debrief: "Imagine climbing a mountain in oppressively humid weather, weighed down by gear, not knowing if there's an entire battalion waiting just over the ridge. That's what Dak To felt like."[8]

Hill Battles and Recon Support

One of the most brutal engagements during this period was the battle for Hill 875 in November 1967. While large American and ARVN units hammered away at entrenched NVA positions, small SOG teams ventured around the base of the hill, identifying infiltration trails the enemy used to bring in reinforcements. Their intelligence allowed U.S. artillery and air power to target those routes, disrupting the flow of supplies and giving allied forces an edge.[9]

In a 1970 interview, Private First Class Nick Townsend recalled a tense infiltration near the foot of Hill 875. His team crept past enemy campsites, praying they wouldn't stumble into a patrol. "We heard them talking—smelled their cooking fires—yet we had to keep pushing forward. Our job was to map out their mortar positions. If they caught us, it wouldn't have ended well."[10] Eventually, their radio transmissions pinpointed the mortar sites, which were then neutralized by air strikes.

Search and Rescue Under Fire

Often, the mountainous environment transformed rescues into heart-stopping endeavors. Helicopters faced anti-aircraft guns hidden along ridges, while landing zones were few and far between. SOG operators collaborated with Air Force pararescue jumpers, sometimes using carefully placed charges to blast out a small clearing for evacuation. The process was perilous: each explosion could attract NVA attention, and the rescue helicopter had to hover at treetop level amid sporadic enemy fire.

Corporal Luis Hernandez, a door gunner aboard a rescue Huey UH-1, described one such mission at Dak To: "We lowered ropes for a wounded SOG team, and all the while, the pilot and I could see muzzle flashes in the tree line. We basically floated there, a perfect target, but we refused to leave until everyone was hauled up. My hand was shaking on the M60 trigger, I was so tense."[11]

Although not as famous in popular memory as larger battles like Khe Sanh or Ia Drang, the Dak To and Kontum campaigns demonstrated the relentless nature of the war in the highlands. For SOG, it was a testament to how small groups—operating discreetly—could tip the balance in engagements that demanded a seamless blend of intelligence, courage, and the ability to traverse punishing landscapes.

The Tet Offensive and SOG's Counteractions

A Countrywide Shock

When the North Vietnamese and VC launched the Tet Offensive on January 30–31, 1968, they aimed to strike at the heart of South Vietnam's cities and towns, including Saigon, Hue, and Da Nang. The offensive came as a jolt to many Americans who believed the conflict was winding down.[12] Overnight, the war spilled into densely populated areas, trapping civilians in the crossfire and forcing commanders to rethink their assumptions about enemy strategy.

Although SOG largely specialized in cross-border missions, the Tet Offensive's broad scope demanded flexibility. Recon teams in border areas had picked up unusual radio chatter and surges in troop movement days prior. Some historians suggest that, had these observations been synthesized rapidly, the offensive might have lost some element of surprise.[13] Regardless, once the attacks commenced, SOG personnel contributed wherever they were needed, including within urban settings.

Transitioning to Urban Terrain

For operators accustomed to blending into thick jungle foliage, operating in a cityscape demanded a whole new approach. Urban structures presented both opportunities and risks: rooftops could serve as vantage points, but enemy snipers also found them ideal for ambush. In Saigon, SOG men joined ad hoc intelligence missions, scouring neighborhoods believed to house VC cells. Disguises were occasionally employed, with some operators adopting civilian clothing to move inconspicuously through crowded streets.[14]

Captain Robert Franks, a SOG officer temporarily seconded to MACV intelligence in Saigon, recalled the mental shift required: "In the jungle, we had ways to disappear into the vegetation. In the city, you couldn't hide

CHARLES J. MCARTHUR

in a bush. You had to adapt to the constant presence of civilians. People might recognize an American face and either help you—or betray you. It added a new layer of tension."[15]

Despite these adjustments, SOG teams managed to feed critical intel about VC safe houses and attack plans to U.S. and ARVN units scrambling to secure strategic buildings. Their infiltration and detailed reporting helped limit the expansion of insurgent footholds in certain districts.

Morale and Aftershocks

For many Americans, the Tet Offensive became a turning point in how they perceived the war. Television footage of gunfire in Saigon's streets and the assault on the U.S. Embassy compound rattled confidence in the prospect of a quick resolution. Morale among U.S. troops was deeply affected. Sergeant Andrew Shelton, in a letter to his sister, remarked, "Tet felt like a storm that never ended. Every day brought more bad news—more chaos in places we thought were secure."[16]

While the allied forces ultimately contained the offensive, it left a profound impression, shaping public opinion back home and fueling debates about the war's direction. For MACV-SOG, Tet underscored the importance of nimble adaptation. A group designed for stealth in remote jungles had just played a role, however modest, in defending major population centers during the biggest coordinated push by the enemy thus far.

Broader Reflections on SOG's Battlefield Impact

Unsung Support and Quiet Heroes

In each of these engagements—Lang Vei, Dak To-Kontum, and the Tet Offensive—SOG's involvement often existed in the margins of official reports. They rarely received headline credit, partly because their missions were covert. Yet those on the ground, whether

American infantry or allied Montagnard fighters, understood how critical SOG's intelligence and specialized assistance could be.

A field artillery officer, who asked to remain anonymous in a 1971 interview, praised SOG recon's role at Dak To: "We'd have been blasting empty jungle a quarter of the time if those teams hadn't guided us. They snuck in close enough to mark enemy positions. Sure, they didn't get the big newspaper stories, but the guys on the front lines knew who to thank."[117]

Adaptation Under Constant Pressure

From tank-led assaults to mountainous firefights and urban ambushes, SOG confronted a broad spectrum of tactical scenarios. Their successes hinged on qualities that defined them: adaptability, precise communication, and an ability to stay calm under extreme danger. This mindset allowed them to maintain relevance in battles that varied widely in scale and terrain.

Even after the dust settled, SOG operators carried with them memories of night engagements, frantic helicopter extractions, and the faces of friends who did not make it home. According to Colonel John Singlaub, "These men served in the shadows, but their impact was very real. And that's the paradox of SOG: the quieter you are, the bigger the difference you can make."[118]

Legacy of These Engagements

In practical terms, the experiences at Lang Vei, Dak To–Kontum, and during Tet forced continuous innovation in tactics and equipment. Faster and more agile helicopters, improved anti-armor measures, and urban infiltration techniques were some of the outcomes. Military planners recognized the value of small, specialized squads that could operate independently, turning lessons learned in these battles into enduring doctrines for future conflicts.

Emotionally, these engagements left scars. SOG operators, like many veterans, wrestled with the psychological weight of close combat. The close calls and tragic losses created a kinship among survivors that lasted well beyond the war. To them, the battles weren't defined by lines on a map or official communiqués; they were marked by muddy foxholes, shattered bunkers, and last-minute rescue flares illuminating a nighttime sky.

Chapter Conclusion

The men of MACV-SOG carved out a distinct role in some of Vietnam's most intense battles and engagements. Whether they were assisting Green Berets under siege at Lang Vei, guiding artillery strikes amid the hills of Dak To, or adapting their jungle-honed skills to an urban battlefield during the Tet Offensive, these operators showed that effectiveness in war isn't always measured in conventional campaigns or sweeping victories. Sometimes it's about acting decisively in a single valley, a single ridge, or a single city block—where the difference between success and disaster might be one recon report, one heroic stand, or one skillful extraction.

In the chapters that follow, we will shed light on the intelligence dimension of SOG's mission—how declassified documents and high-stakes espionage fed into the broader war effort. While battles like Lang Vei, Dak To, and the Tet Offensive tested SOG's resilience on the ground, the secrets uncovered through intelligence often determined which fights would be waged in the first place. Together, these facets illustrate a conflict that extended far beyond the gunshots we see in archival footage, revealing a complex tapestry woven by covert and conventional forces alike.

Chapter 8

The Intelligence War, the Phoenix Program, and Declassified Insights

T hroughout the Vietnam War, intelligence served as the lifeblood of covert operations. Whether it involved identifying high-level VC officers or uncovering enemy weapons caches in remote jungles, accurate information made the difference between success and disaster. MACV-SOG played a pivotal role in this shadowy battle, working alongside various U.S. agencies—including the CIA—and complementing larger initiatives such as the Phoenix Program. Over time, newly declassified documents have revealed the depth of SOG's involvement in intelligence-gathering, counterinsurgency, and targeted actions designed to erode the VC's clandestine infrastructure. This chapter explores those revelations, the ethical quandaries they pose, and the operational strategies that defined the hidden front of the Vietnam conflict.

Collection Methods and Counterintelligence: The SOG—CIA Nexus

Multi-Agency Collaboration

From the outset, SOG existed in a realm where lines between military and intelligence operations blurred. While the unit formally fell under the umbrella of MACV, many of its directives and operational details emerged through close coordination with the CIA.

Publicly, the Agency maintained an advisory role, but newly released files (e.g., CIA Archive #CIA-VN-67-103) confirm that CIA officers and SOG recon teams often collaborated on joint missions across the borders of Laos and Cambodia, sharing methods to conceal U.S. footprints.[1]

One reason for this synergy was that both organizations recognized a fundamental reality: winning in Vietnam required more than large-scale battles; it demanded penetrating the communist networks and undermining the VC's capacity to move and communicate. A 1967 CIA briefing, partially declassified in 2020, states, "Conventional military power can degrade the enemy's overt forces, but infiltration of their political and logistical cells requires specialized methods. SOG's competencies offer a unique complement to CIA paramilitary efforts."[2]

Linking HUMINT, SIGINT, and Psychological Operations

Both the CIA and SOG recognized the necessity of combining multiple intelligence disciplines. Human intelligence (HUMINT) was crucial for infiltrating VC cells or obtaining first-hand information from defectors. Meanwhile, signals intelligence (SIGINT) helped eavesdrop on enemy transmissions and track movement along the Ho Chi Minh Trail. SOG contributed specialized ground reconnaissance, gleaning fresh data on enemy ambush sites or base areas that improved CIA analyses in Saigon.

Together, the agencies also employed psychological tactics to mislead or disrupt VC operations. Operation Eldest Son—discussed earlier—exemplified SOG's talent for sowing fear among enemy ranks by sabotaging ammunition and ran right up to 1971 when MACV-SOG HQ pulled out of Vietnam. Eldon Bargewell, now back on his 2nd Vietnam tour said "So I became the team leader again after

the first mission for the rest of my tour in
SOG, which ended in September '72. I ran, I
think, eight missions eight or nine missions.
On the eighth one, I got shot up real bad. And
so I was out of action for like six weeks. Team
didn't do anything until I healed up. And then
I run a couple of more. And then by about
December, end of November, December '71
is when MACV and MACV-SOG headquarters
shut down running the missions. And that's it,
no more missions"[3] Newly available CIA cables
reference how the Agency saw "parallels
between SOG's approach to psychological
disruption and the CIA's ongoing efforts
under the Phoenix Program," suggesting that
certain psychological warfare strategies were
shared or tested jointly.[4]

Counterintelligence Challenges

Inside this intricate web of clandestine
operations, counterintelligence posed
persistent difficulties. VC spies infiltrated
South Vietnamese units, while the communist
leadership adeptly concealed its networks

within civilian populations. SOG faced the additional burden of ensuring that local interpreters, guides, or allied militia were not double agents. According to a 1968 SOG field report (RG 472, Box 58, partially declassified in 2021), the unit uncovered at least two infiltration attempts by VC sympathizers seeking to join recon teams in the Central Highlands.[5] These incidents spurred more rigorous vetting, sometimes involving CIA background checks or polygraph assessments.

However, the clandestine nature of these missions meant that intelligence only circulated among a tight circle of SOG operators and high-level agency officials. This secrecy reduced the risk of leaks but also made it difficult to confirm or refute allegations of wrongdoing. When rumors surfaced that certain SOG-led raids had targeted civilians or non-combatants, official denials proved difficult to verify due to the closed-loop flow of sensitive data.

The Phoenix Program: A Controversial Counterinsurgency Tool

Origins and Overlaps with SOG

Launched in 1967, the Phoenix Program (Phung Hoang in Vietnamese) aimed to dismantle the VC's clandestine political infrastructure by identifying, capturing, or neutralizing key operatives. Overseen by the CIA in concert with South Vietnamese agencies, Phoenix used a mix of intelligence-gathering, interrogation, and local informants to strike at the insurgent leadership from within. While Phoenix officially fell outside SOG's purview, declassified cables indicate that SOG recon teams occasionally provided intelligence that guided Phoenix operations, especially in remote areas where conventional intelligence assets struggled to operate.[6]

For instance, a newly released 1969 CIA field memorandum (File #CIA-PHX-69-045) reveals how a SOG team in the Kontum region intercepted a VC courier carrying lists of suspected collaborators. This intel was handed off to Phoenix Program coordinators, who then launched targeted arrests in provincial towns. Though SOG's focus remained on deep recon and sabotage, such handovers highlight the synergy between the two agencies' covert work.

The main objectives of Operation Phoenix were:

- **Identification of VC Infrastructure (VCI) Members:** Phoenix sought to identify individuals who were part of the VCI, including political operatives, logistics personnel, and other civilians who supported the VC's military efforts.

- **Neutralization of the VCI:** Once identified, VCI members were to be "neutralized," which meant they could be captured, interrogated, imprisoned, or killed. The term "neutralization" was deliberately vague, allowing for a wide range of actions, including assassination.

- **Disruption of VC Operations:** By dismantling the VCI, Phoenix aimed to disrupt the flow of supplies, intelligence, and recruits to the VC's military forces, thereby weakening the insurgency.

- **Counterintelligence and Infiltration:** Phoenix operatives worked to infiltrate the VCI by recruiting informants, defectors, and double agents who could provide intelligence on the insurgency's activities and leadership.[7]

Figure 15 – Original Patch used by the Phoenix Program Operatives (note the 13 laurel leaves of Roman Dynastical symbology carried through into the CIA by the likes of Director Allen Dulles, A 'Knight of Malta')

Methods and Moral Controversies

The Phoenix Program has long been a lightning rod of controversy, criticized for alleged abuses including torture during interrogation and extrajudicial killings. While official Phoenix documents stress the aim of "neutralizing" communist infrastructure, critics assert the program often crossed ethical and legal lines. SOG's involvement was generally indirect, as SOG teams lacked the local policing authority that Phoenix field teams and South Vietnamese security forces wielded. Nevertheless, the intelligence they supplied sometimes fed into a system known for its harsh interrogation tactics.

The Phoenix Program can be viewed as a modern iteration of the same principles that governed ancient Rome's counterinsurgency strategies: control through covert networks, the delegation of power to local forces, and ruthless suppression of dissent. No wonder, as CIA founding directors were also Knights of The Sovereign Order of Malta. The Knights of Malta trace their origins to the Knights Hospitaller, a medieval Catholic military order formed during the Crusades. These orders echoed aspects of Roman militarized religious loyalty (e.g., devotion to the state-religion of Rome) and incorporated ancient Roman traditions of maintaining elite, covert influence over frontier regions. This could be why the Roman Laurels are depicted in the Phoenix Programme patch.

Sergeant Willis Beck, who served as an intelligence liaison between SOG and the CIA, recounted in a private 1974 interview (partially declassified in 2022) how "we'd pass along targeting data for certain VC figures that local Phoenix teams were after. We hoped it'd lead to legit captures or forced defections. Whether those suspects were treated fairly was not in our control, but the moral weight still lingered."[8] This admission underscores the complexities for SOG operators who contributed to a broader program that wielded questionable methods.

Newly Declassified Reports and Unseen Dimensions

Recent declassifications from the CIA (Archive #CIA-PHX-70-201) paint a fuller picture of the operational overlap between SOG and Phoenix. In one late-1970 memo, a CIA station chief acknowledged the importance of SOG recon intel: "Route interdictions by MACV-SOG hamper enemy movement, thereby funneling key cadres into areas where Phoenix assets operate. This synergy has resulted in heightened captures of mid-level communist agents."[9] While the memo praises the results, it also cites concerns about how the Phoenix Program's "paramilitary intensity" could backfire if local populations perceived it as overly punitive.

These revelations show that while Phoenix and SOG remained distinct entities with different mandates, their paths intersected enough to significantly influence Vietnam's covert conflict. Whether this synergy advanced or undermined overall war aims remains a matter of debate among historians, given the moral controversies that still hover around Phoenix.

Newly Declassified Intelligence Findings

MACV-SOG After-Action Reports: CIA Collaboration

The U.S. National Archives have recently released a series of SOG after-action reports (RG 472, Boxes 75–77) revealing how intelligence collected from cross-border missions frequently made its way to CIA analysts. These reports detail instances where SOG recon teams in Laos encountered not just NVA regulars but also "political commissars" assigned to maintain morale among troops. This detail—apparently overlooked by standard Army intelligence—proved invaluable to CIA officers tracking the ideological backbone of the NVA.[10]

One 1968 SOG summary notes: "Interrogation of a captured commissar indicates growing discipline issues in certain NVA battalions. Morale is strained by supply shortages and increased infiltration hazards. CIA station Saigon notified for potential exploitation of psychological vulnerabilities."[11] Historians see this as a prime example of how SOG's tactical successes shaped strategic intelligence that was, in turn, funneled into broader campaigns like Phoenix or psychological warfare programs.

CIA's Counterintelligence Gains

Another newly declassified set of CIA cables (Archive #CIA-VN-70-099) references clandestine captures orchestrated by combined SOG and Phoenix elements. In these cables, CIA operatives praise SOG for identifying routes used by higher-level VC couriers. The CIA and Phoenix teams subsequently established ambushes in South Vietnamese villages near the border, "significantly disrupting the VC's internal communication chain for an estimated 5–6 weeks."[12]

Yet these documents also hint at friction between CIA paramilitaries and SOG recon teams over how to handle detainees. While SOG was typically authorized to gather intelligence in the field and then exfiltrate, the CIA's paramilitary arm sometimes pushed for immediate, harsh interrogation to glean real-time leads, often interrogating innocent civilians on questionable intelligence. This tension exemplifies a broader schism: SOG's mission primarily targeted supply lines and direct intelligence, while Phoenix's mission was more focused on *political* subversion and infiltration with a leaning toward direct assassination of political figures. The CIA's own records cited around 20,587 'eliminations' as of 1971, with other estimates increasing that number by the end of the program.

Operational Revelations on Cross-Border Tactics

A final cluster of declassified records underscores the importance of advanced infiltration techniques. CIA training manuals show that SOG operators received additional instruction on "urban infiltration" and "rural political mapping" for certain missions close to population centers—a skill set more in line with Phoenix infiltration tactics.[13] The revelations complicate earlier narratives that SOG exclusively operated in jungles and border zones, suggesting that some teams occasionally ventured into semi-urban or densely populated enclaves in pursuit of high-value targets.

In a 1971 CIA debriefing, a SOG operator identified as "Raven" described posing as a traveling merchant in a border town near Cambodia, scouting out local VC political officers who oversaw taxation and conscription. The intelligence gleaned led to a Phoenix-led crackdown that captured at least three mid-level VC political cadres.[14] While small in scale, these results underscore the integrated nature of the intelligence war, where CIA infiltration tactics, SOG's special operations flair, and Phoenix's local enforcement combined.

Key Intelligence Breakthroughs and Ethical Implications

Targeting High-Value Cadres

SOG's cross-border recon often unearthed the presence of high-level communist cadres guiding insurgent strategies. Declassified Phoenix files (#PHX-69-202) confirm that SOG tip-offs facilitated at least a dozen raids that captured or eliminated VC district chiefs and political commissars. Some of these cadres oversaw elaborate underground networks, controlling propaganda, local militias, and logistical webs that sustained the insurgency.[15]

The swift removal of such leaders sometimes had an outsized impact, delaying VC offensives or fracturing local insurgent hierarchies. However, critics argue this approach—particularly under Phoenix—risked conflating genuine insurgent leaders with minor functionaries or innocents mislabeled by paid informants. As a result, while SOG provided the "heads-up" intel, the subsequent arrests or eliminations could devolve into questionable or abusive actions at the hands of local authorities.

The Cost of Secrecy

The same secrecy that ensured operational security also obscured accountability. Families of detainees taken under Phoenix sweeps rarely received clear answers. SOG operators, for their part, often learned of a detainee's fate secondhand or not at all. Sergeant Harold Elkins, speaking in 1988, mentioned how "we'd deliver intel about a certain cadre, but never knew how Phoenix resolved it. Sometimes you'd hear rumors a suspect vanished or ended up at a camp. It could gnaw at you, wondering whether we had fingered the right person."[16]

This dissonance between the front-line gatherers of intelligence (SOG) and the implementers of harsh interrogation or lethal measures (Phoenix and associated ARVN units) contributed to lingering guilt among some SOG veterans. Newly released personal letters and diaries reveal a subtle but ongoing internal debate: Did the ends justify the means in a war fought largely in the dark?

Shaping Future Doctrine

Despite such controversies, the intelligence breakthroughs that SOG and CIA-Phoenix collaboration achieved undeniably altered the Vietnam War's trajectory, at least temporarily. By revealing how deeply the VC had infiltrated rural communities, the operations forced communist cells to move more cautiously and adopt new communication protocols. In turn, these shifts taught U.S. strategists valuable lessons about the interconnectedness of military, political, and psychological fronts in a guerrilla war—lessons that would inform future conflicts from Central America to the Middle East.

Chapter Conclusion: A Complex Legacy

The intelligence war that MACV-SOG waged alongside the CIA and the Phoenix Program stands as one of the Vietnam conflict's most intricate chapters. On one level, it demonstrated how specialized reconnaissance and targeted operations could disrupt a well-entrenched insurgency by denying it leadership and logistical freedom. On another level, it revealed the moral and ethical pitfalls of clandestine methods—particularly those that skirted the boundaries of international law and democratic oversight.

The synergy between SOG and Phoenix:

- **SOG**: Provided in-field recon, sabotage, and direct action behind enemy lines.

- **Phoenix**: Leveraged local informants, interrogation, and counterinsurgency policing to dismantle VC political structures.

- **CIA**: Acted as a bridging force, facilitating intelligence exchange, infiltration training, and funding for paramilitary efforts.

As newly declassified records come to light, the depth of this collaboration becomes increasingly apparent. The glimpses we have into cross-border missions, captured VC dossiers, and Phoenix-led roundups underscore the multi-layered nature of the Vietnam War's covert dimension. Yet these same revelations invite ongoing scrutiny about the methods employed. For veterans of SOG who contributed data or directly assisted Phoenix operations, the question remains whether the valuable intelligence gleaned was worth the moral toll of enabling a program fraught with allegations of abuse.

In the final accounting, MACV-SOG's intelligence war illuminates both the promise and peril of clandestine operations. Effective in short-term disruption, it also taught that intelligence alone cannot resolve the fundamental political and social grievances fueling an insurgency. As we turn to the next chapter, we will examine the broader ethical debates and controversies that these covert missions inevitably stirred, offering a window into the moral crossroads faced by those who served in the shadows.

Chapter 9

Ethical Debates and Controversies

Covert warfare often stands at the crossroads of conflicting demands—military necessity, political objectives, and moral responsibility. In the case of MACV-SOG, these tensions became particularly acute. Operating largely in the shadows, SOG teams executed sensitive missions in areas where official policy claimed no American presence. While many of their actions were applauded by military leadership for their effectiveness, critics both inside and outside the U.S. government raised challenging questions about ethics, legality, and the potential cost to civilians. This chapter delves into some of the key controversies surrounding SOG's operations, highlighting the internal and external debates that continue to shape how we perceive their role in the Vietnam conflict.

Figure 16 – SOG Hatchet members readying for Operation Tailwind, 1970.

Covert Operations vs. Public Accountability

Political Ramifications of Secrecy

From its inception, MACV-SOG was designed to conduct missions that, if made public, could trigger international outcry or escalate tensions with neighboring countries like Laos and Cambodia.[1] Consequently, mission reports were classified at the highest levels, and few outside a select circle of policymakers and military commanders possessed full knowledge of these incursions. This secrecy had a profound impact on governance and democracy: how could lawmakers provide oversight for operations that officially "did not exist"?

In a 1973 Senate subcommittee hearing—later partially declassified—one senator pressed a Defense Department official on whether the American public had a right to know about covert missions being carried out in their name. The official carefully skirted specifics, citing "national security," which only fueled suspicions of a hidden war. Major David Porter, a SOG intelligence officer at the time, would reflect decades later: "We had to keep telling the field teams to limit who they talked to. We worried someone would blow the lid on these missions. In hindsight, it's easy to see how that secrecy created distrust."[2]

Cross-Border Raids and Denials

Among the most contentious aspects of SOG's work were its cross-border raids into countries that were officially neutral. Publicly, U.S. spokespeople insisted America respected territorial boundaries. Internally, strategic planners deemed these raids essential to interdict the Ho Chi Minh Trail. A once-classified briefing from 1967 spelled out the rationale: "Enemy supply routes know no borders. Denying the adversary's logistical network is paramount to success."[3]

Yet by denying these incursions, U.S. leaders exposed themselves to claims of deception when evidence of SOG's presence trickled out. In 1970, journalists obtained leaked documents showing dramatic inconsistencies between official statements and actual operations.[4] For soldiers on the ground, this denial meant they had to operate under constant risk of political fallout, even if their immediate concern was avoiding capture or ambush. Some, like Sergeant Patrick Lin, expressed unease: "We knew we were in places we weren't supposed to be. We just hoped that if something went wrong, we wouldn't be disowned."[5]

Collateral Damage and Civilian Concerns

The Human Cost of Sabotage

Many of SOG's missions focused on sabotaging enemy supply lines, sometimes by mining roads or seeding booby-trapped ammunition (as in Operation Eldest Son). While these actions could disrupt North Vietnamese logistics, they also raised ethical questions about potential harm to civilians. A farmer using the same road for market trade or a local who innocently stumbled upon a rigged cache might become an unintended casualty.

Staff Sergeant Lewis Gaunt, interviewed in 1990, remembered wrestling with the moral implications: "We'd set charges on truck routes. We tried to time them for when only enemy convoys were moving, but you couldn't always know who else might come along."[6] Declassified after-action reports occasionally hint at cases where non-combatants were injured. Although not extensive, these incidents added to the moral burden operators carried, knowing the line between legitimate targets and unintended victims could blur in clandestine warfare.

Destruction of Resources and Local Livelihoods

SOG teams also burned or destroyed enemy stockpiles—rice stores, livestock pens, or huts storing weapons. While the destruction of war materiel was consistent with military objectives, critics argued it risked eroding the support of neutral or ambivalent villagers. Some local communities already distrusted both sides, and these scorched-earth tactics, even if justified by the presence of enemy supplies, could tip them toward resentment.

In a private 1969 journal entry, Lieutenant Dominic Castelli of a SOG recon unit mentioned stumbling upon a small settlement that looked largely abandoned: "We set charges on a weapons stash. Later, I wondered if those huts had been home to innocents, forced out by the fighting. I knew we were just doing our job, but the ghosts lingered."[7] Stories like these, pieced together from diaries and letters, remind us that covert campaigns often intersect with the ordinary lives of people simply trying to survive.

Treatment of Prisoners and POW Rescues

Interrogation and Rumors of Harsh Methods

The capture of enemy personnel sometimes yielded valuable intelligence. However, SOG's remit included interrogation practices that, while not officially endorsed as torture, dwelled in a gray area. Some operators took pains to stay within the moral high ground, using psychologically oriented questioning or reliance on language experts to glean insights. Others, however, are alleged—based on veteran testimonies—to have employed more coercive tactics under pressure to produce results quickly.[8]

Official records remain sparse or heavily redacted on this issue, reflecting the topic's sensitivity. A 1974 Army Inspector General's report did uncover allegations of inappropriate treatment in at least two SOG-run field camps, but the outcomes of any investigations remain largely unknown.[9] Many veterans, when asked, either deny personal involvement or say they witnessed only humane questioning techniques.

High-Stakes POW Rescues

Conversely, SOG teams often risked their lives to rescue American prisoners of war, a goal that typically commanded wide moral support. The most famous example is the Son Tay Raid in 1970, planned in large part using intelligence from SOG sources.[10] Though the raid discovered that the POWs had been moved, the bold attempt spotlighted SOG's willingness to gamble everything on missions to save captured comrades.

Sergeant William "Steel" Martin, who served in SOG and later joined the Son Tay planning staff, described the emotional drive behind such operations: "We'd all heard stories of guys taken captive and feared the worst. When we planned Son Tay, it felt like the entire unit wanted to volunteer. None of us hesitated, even knowing the odds might be stacked against us."[11] These rescue endeavors highlight a more human dimension to the covert war—one that balanced aggression with an unwavering sense of loyalty.

Ethical Dilemmas in Extreme Conditions

Balancing Survival and Morality

On the ground, MACV-SOG operators operated under intense conditions: infiltration miles behind enemy lines, the threat of capture, and the knowledge that any slip in secrecy could doom them. The boundary between pure survival and ethical restraint was sometimes razor-thin. In a 1978 oral history, Specialist Roger Leeds recalled a mission in Laos: "We were cut off, running low on ammo, starving. One of our guys suggested raiding a local village for food. Another refused, said we'd lose our last shred of decency. We argued for hours in whispers, all the while expecting the enemy to close in."[12]

Such episodes underline the inner conflicts faced by small teams. Even without formal orders to commit unethical acts, desperation could push them toward decisions they might regret. That many SOG veterans struggled to talk about these incidents afterward underscores the emotional weight they carried. It is estimated that over 50 MACV-SOG operators are still listed as missing in action to this day – their bodies never found. Eldon Bargewell commented "I went on a few [Op] Bright Lights that were unsuccessful and the fact, we could never find the guys and later found out that they'd been killed. And the NVA had buried them someplace. And some of them were found. Some of them have never been found. I think my SOG unit, CCN, CCC, CCS still have 50 people missing.[13] After Vietnam, Eldon continued service, passing selection and serving with Delta Force (rising to Delta unit commander), and eventually retiring as a Major General in 2007. He sadly died, aged 71, in 2019.

Friendly Fire and Inter-Unit Tensions

SOG's unconventional tactics required close coordination with regular forces and allied Vietnamese troops to avoid confusion. Miscommunication sometimes led to friendly fire incidents. An ex-SOG operator, who asked to remain unnamed in a 1985 interview, described a tragic event: "Our team was pinned down near the border. We called for air support, but the pilots mixed up our coordinates and dropped ordnance too close.

One of our Montagnard scouts died that night, and I could never shake the guilt."[14]

Beyond the sheer sadness of losing compatriots, such missteps eroded trust among different branches of the military. Critiques arose that SOG's secrecy caused misunderstandings, with conventional units rarely fully informed about clandestine operations happening within their sector. Repeated slip-ups fueled internal debates on whether the veil of secrecy did more harm than good, both for operations and inter-service relationships.

Post-War Criticisms and Reflection

Veteran Accounts and Regrets

Long after the conflict's end, some SOG veterans expressed regrets. In oral histories recorded in the 1980s and 1990s, a recurring theme was the question: "Did we cross lines we shouldn't have?" The testimonies vary—many insisted their missions were necessary to save American and South Vietnamese lives, while others acknowledged the conflict's broader moral ambiguities.

Staff Sergeant Tina Morales, one of the few female administrative clerks attached to SOG, wrote in her memoir that she overheard many tormented conversations: "They'd come back from a raid, sit down, and talk in hushed tones about seeing children in the village. They never wanted to hurt civilians, but war rarely gave them that clear choice."[15] For some, reconciling their sense of duty with the ethical gray areas of clandestine operations proved a lifelong struggle.

Government Acknowledgment and Public Debate

As partial declassifications began in the 1980s, more details of MACV-SOG's operations came to light. This prompted new debates about whether the government should have permitted—or concealed—missions that risked diplomatic crises and potentially jeopardized civilian lives.[16] Congressional hearings intermittently revisited these concerns, although by then public interest in the Vietnam War had waned. Still, for historians, veterans, and ethicists, these revelations fueled ongoing scrutiny of how far a nation should go in covert warfare.

Ultimately, SOG's example has informed policy discussions in subsequent conflicts, where concerns about transparency, rules of engagement, and collateral damage remain front and center. In this sense, the controversies surrounding SOG resonated beyond Vietnam, shaping future standards and prompting deeper inquiries into the intersection of secrecy and accountability.

Chapter Conclusion

The story of MACV-SOG is impossible to understand without acknowledging the ethical controversies that accompanied its high-risk missions. Operating clandestinely in multiple countries, these teams took extraordinary measures to hamper a determined enemy. Yet the very methods that ensured success—covert raids, sabotage campaigns, ambiguous rules of engagement—also placed them in moral dilemmas. Civilians, prisoners, and local communities sometimes bore the brunt of actions conceived in the name of strategic necessity.

Their experiences speak to the harrowing complexities of covert warfare. Time and again, SOG operators grappled with impossible decisions under life-threatening constraints. Some emerged with a sense of pride in having shielded friendly forces from harm; others carried unresolved questions about the moral costs of achieving those objectives. Today, as more documents become public and veterans share their stories, the netting of SOG's legacy grows more intricate. These revelations remind us that behind every top-secret mission lie individuals wrestling with issues of conscience, responsibility, and humanity—issues that still challenge military institutions and societies around the world.

Chapter 10

Legacy, Lessons Learned, and Modern Relevance

A s the Vietnam War drew to an uneasy close in 1975, the covert efforts of MACV-SOG—together with other highly secret initiatives like the Phoenix Program—faded behind layers of classification. Only years later did details emerge, thanks to veterans' testimonies, partial declassifications, and historical inquiry. In examining these revelations, one finds that SOG's influence on U.S. military doctrine far outlived the conflict itself, shaping how modern special operations operate and how policymakers weigh the moral complexities of clandestine warfare. This chapter explores the broad legacy of MACV-SOG, re-examining the lessons gleaned from their partnership with intelligence entities, including the Phoenix Program, and assessing their enduring relevance in contemporary conflicts worldwide.

Evolution of U.S. Special Operations Post-Vietnam

The Shift Toward Organizational Cohesion

In the immediate aftermath of the Vietnam War, the U.S. military underwent a period of self-reflection. The conflict had revealed the limits of mass conventional deployments in a region where an elusive enemy and complicated political realities demanded subtler solutions. Meanwhile, clandestine efforts—ranging from SOG's cross-border missions to the Phoenix Program's targeted neutralizations—showed that carefully orchestrated small-unit and intelligence-driven approaches could disrupt enemy networks significantly, albeit at ethical and political costs.

These insights helped catalyze the formation of the United States Special Operations Command (SOCOM) in 1987, which consolidated various elite units under a unified structure.[1] Lessons gleaned from MACV-SOG's fluid, multi-agency ethos—and from the CIA-backed Phoenix Program—reinforced that special operations function best when guided by agile command relationships and robust intelligence sharing. Veterans of SOG, as well as intelligence operators who had worked on Phoenix, brought experiences that shaped SOCOM's emphasis on integrating small-unit reconnaissance, psychological operations, and specialized direct actions.

Incorporating the Phoenix Model into Doctrine

The Phoenix Program's influence on counterinsurgency doctrine also trickled into post-Vietnam thinking. Though publicly criticized for alleged abuses, Phoenix underscored how dismantling insurgent political cells could prove as crucial as targeting main-force units. In the 1980s and 1990s, U.S. Army and joint-service manuals began to include sections on "high-value targeting" and "strategic decapitation," echoing Phoenix's fundamental principle of neutralizing key enemy personnel.[2]

For special operations, the synergy between intelligence (via the CIA) and on-the-ground units (like SOG or other specialized outfits) became a key blueprint for future conflicts. Whether tackling drug cartels in Latin America or terrorist networks in the Middle East, the U.S. leaned on a model that combined covert infiltration with refined targeting procedures—always hovering at the edge of moral and legal debate. Thus, one sees how the Phoenix Program and SOG's mission sets overlapped in an intellectual continuum that shaped later doctrinal practices.

Monumental Courage and Sacrifice

Memorials, Reunions, and Family Acknowledgment

Because secrecy shrouded their actions for decades, many SOG operators (and Phoenix collaborators) received delayed recognition for their bravery. It wasn't until the 1980s and early 1990s—when portions of the Vietnam archive were declassified—that family members fully grasped the heroics or sacrifices their loved ones had made. Official ceremonies began awarding commendations to veterans who had previously gone unrecognized. Meanwhile, unit reunions offered a supportive environment where individuals could reconnect and process shared traumas.

For SOG especially, the passage of time allowed operators to speak more openly. At Special Forces gatherings, they recalled the hair-raising cross-border raids, the near-fatal firefights, and the moral quandaries that lingered when intelligence led to lethal outcomes. Often, they discovered parallels in the experiences of Phoenix veterans who struggled with ethical concerns about targeted neutralization and allegations of civilian harm.

Figure 17 –
The Special Warfare
Memorial Statue, Fort
Bragg

Honoring Phoenix Program Contributors

Though overshadowed by controversies, many who participated in Phoenix likewise demonstrated dedication and courage, risking their lives to infiltrate VC political networks. In some ways, they were as vulnerable as SOG recon teams—operating in villages rife with insurgent sympathies, never certain who might betray them. While the program's reputation remains clouded by allegations of abuse, those who served honorably within it also share stories of friendship, life-saving tips gleaned from local informants, and narrow escapes akin to those recounted by SOG members in remote jungles.

The Shared Emotional Toll

A significant aspect of SOG's and Phoenix's combined story lies in the emotional aftermath. Missions that hinged on secrecy left many veterans feeling disconnected upon returning home, unable to explain their experiences due to classification constraints. Some wrestled with guilt or unresolved grief, particularly when intelligence they provided led to uncertain fates for detainees or communities. Newly compiled oral histories reveal that veterans often found closure only decades later—when they realized their moral struggles were neither unique nor unshared. They had shouldered the burden of covert war so that others might remain ignorant of the brutal undercurrents shaping U.S. policy.

Actionable Lessons for Future Generations

Leadership Under Pressure and Cross-Agency Synergy

SOG was known for cultivating leaders at every rank, trusting small teams to solve complex problems under extreme conditions. The Phoenix Program, though more intelligence-driven, similarly relied on mid-level officers and field agents who had to improvise under fluid political circumstances—whether in a crowded village or a clandestine interrogation site. In both cases, leaders often operated with minimal oversight from higher command, forging crucial decisions with minimal guidance.

Modern special operations, from the post-9/11 conflicts to more recent advisory missions in Africa and Asia, have embraced this leadership model. The emphasis on synergy between small-unit operators and intelligence resources reflects the SOG–Phoenix interplay: agile, localized decision-making supplemented by national-level intelligence. This approach proved pivotal in missions like the early Afghanistan campaign (2001–2002) and various global counterterrorism efforts, where lethal strikes against high-value targets (HVTs) could shift battlefield dynamics rapidly.[13]

CHARLES J. MCARTHUR

Intelligence, Targeting, and Ethical Constraints

SOG's infiltration missions and Phoenix's infiltration of VC political structures jointly underscore how intelligence can be a double-edged sword. Effective intel can disrupt enemy networks with minimal force, but it can also open the door to abuses if checks and balances are weak. Post-Vietnam reforms attempted to codify targeting procedures, demanding more thorough vetting before lethal or coercive actions. Yet debates persist—especially when U.S. forces operate in legally ambiguous environments.

While successive doctrines incorporate lessons about transparency and accountability, the tension remains. If intelligence is central to shaping operations, how do modern militaries ensure moral lines aren't crossed under secrecy's cloak? MACV-SOG's direct experience with cross-border raids and Phoenix's political targeting illustrate

216

the perils of unrestrained covert action. Contemporary intelligence-driven operations—like drone-based strikes or "kill-capture" missions—walk the same razor's edge: potential tactical success offset by strategic or moral blowback.

The Importance of Psychological Resilience

Both SOG and Phoenix introduced new forms of psychological strain: from SOG operators fearing capture with no official acknowledgment to Phoenix officers confronting the moral weight of infiltration and possible abuses in interrogation facilities. Modern militaries, having learned from Vietnam veterans' experiences, now integrate mental health services more thoroughly into special operations planning. Tier-one units often deploy with embedded mental health professionals, and post-deployment psychological evaluations aim to catch early signs of trauma or moral injury.

This ongoing attention to mental health stands as a direct legacy of Vietnam-era lessons. The U.S. military recognized—albeit gradually—that psychological support is not a luxury but a necessity for sustaining elite forces that engage in morally ambiguous and intensely stressful operations. Sergeant James Monroe, a SOG recon leader, once wrote in a private letter that "some nights I'd dream about the men we couldn't rescue or the detainee who might've been innocent. War is war, but the images stay."[4] Today, that raw testimony informs mental health frameworks across special ops units worldwide.

Contemporary Relevance

Applications in Modern Conflicts

The synergy between direct-action raids (à la SOG) and targeted intelligence-led programs (inspired by Phoenix) resonates in contemporary missions from the Middle East to Africa. Joint Special Operations Task Forces often combine operators capable of covert infiltration with robust intelligence cells that identify and track insurgent or terrorist networks. For example, in Iraq and Afghanistan, high-value target hunts have integrated signals intelligence (SIGINT), human intelligence (HUMINT), and drone surveillance—echoing the multi-faceted approach SOG and Phoenix once employed.

Moreover, "nation-building" or "advisory" components in modern conflicts also recall the Phoenix Program's efforts to stand up local security and gather local intelligence—though with (ideally) tighter oversight. Commanders remain aware that local partnerships can yield potent outcomes but also risk blowback if poorly managed, given that local forces might engage in reprisals or corruption under the cover of U.S. operations. This tension mirrors the controversies that dogged Phoenix's reliance on ARVN and regional police units, where infiltration or personal vendettas sometimes tarnished the program's broader goals.[5]

Legal and Ethical Restraints

Vietnam's covert wars exposed how official denials and classification barriers can shield questionable practices from public scrutiny. Modern operations now often involve legal frameworks—like Status of Forces Agreements (SOFAs) or congressional oversight committees—designed to prevent the reemergence of "unaccountable warfare." Yet even these measures can prove porous in rapidly evolving conflicts. Cases like the CIA's enhanced interrogation controversies post-9/11 highlight how moral hazards reemerge when intelligence agencies and special units coordinate in legal gray zones.

Thus, SOG and Phoenix's legacy remains a cautionary tale. While they proved effective at specific tactical aims—disrupting supply lines, dismantling insurgent structures—they also underscored the risk of losing public support or moral high ground if secret missions stray beyond acceptable conduct. This duality forces present-day planners to weigh each covert initiative's strategic payoff against the potential fallout should misconduct or collateral damage become public.

Influences on Global Special Forces Communities

It isn't just the U.S. that learned from SOG and Phoenix. Allied nations' special forces—like the British Special Air Service (SAS) or Australian SASR—also studied the Vietnam War's covert methods. These forces integrated relevant tactics for small-team reconnaissance and infiltration within their own doctrines. Global "counterinsurgency academies" have likewise referenced Phoenix Program insights into dismantling insurgent leadership, while cautioning about the program's human rights controversies.

In essence, SOG's small-unit operations, combined with Phoenix's intelligence-driven targeting, collectively shaped an enduring model for irregular warfare. Whether it's a European special forces unit tackling hostage rescues in Africa or an Asian counterterrorism brigade hunting militant cells, they're drawing on a lineage that includes Vietnam's covert battles—often acknowledging the moral complexities embedded within.

Balancing Heroism, Morality, and Secrecy

The Dilemma of Public Accountability

Even decades later, the tension lingers between the necessity for secrecy and the democratic principle of transparency. At times, officials during Vietnam denied the very existence of cross-border SOG missions and Phoenix's infiltration efforts, only for the truth to surface years later. In modern contexts, too, classification can conceal how lethal decisions are made—particularly if they involve foreign territories or targeted eliminations of suspected insurgent leaders.

Advocates argue that secrecy can prevent tipping off the enemy and protect operators' lives, while critics note that excessive secrecy can breed abuses and shield policy failures. The SOG–Phoenix experience highlights how both can be true: secrecy does enhance operational security, yet it can also erode accountability. This conundrum persists in debates around drone strikes, black-site prisons, and special operations missions worldwide.

Reconciling Past Controversies

For veterans of SOG and Phoenix, reconciling their roles remains a personal journey. Some take pride in having saved lives by crippling the VC's ability to wage war, while others express lingering doubts about whether clandestine missions or detainee interrogations strayed into unethical terrain. Public interest in the Vietnam War's covert side has sparked new scholarship and documentary projects, giving these veterans a platform to share nuanced reflections and clarifications.

In 2003, a series of panel discussions—dubbed "Invisible Warriors: Vietnam's Secret

Front"—brought together ex-SOG operators and former Phoenix case officers. Transcripts reveal that while heated disagreements arose, participants found solace in acknowledging shared burdens and complexities. Sergeant William "Doc" Garner, an ex-SOG medic, commented, "We all did things that have haunted us, but we also prevented what could have been greater bloodshed. There's no clean corner in that war, but maybe talking helps us see the bigger picture."

Potential Paths Forward

Modern militaries looking to avoid Vietnam's pitfalls must craft robust oversight mechanisms that address both moral and operational imperatives. That might include clearer legal frameworks for covert ops, pre-mission ethical reviews, or dedicated ombudsmen to track allegations of misconduct. Equally important is ensuring that intelligence-driven programs—like Phoenix—incorporate stringent vetting, transparency about detainee treatment, and local community engagement to prevent alienation or backlash. While these reforms may never fully eliminate risk, they reflect an evolved awareness rooted in SOG and Phoenix's storied past.

Chapter Conclusion: A Legacy Carried into the Shadows—and the Light

When historians recount MACV-SOG's achievements, they often speak of the high-risk reconnaissance and sabotage that tested the limits of human endurance in Vietnam's jungles. Yet SOG's legacy cannot be separated from its interwoven relationship with intelligence agencies, nor from the Phoenix Program's contentious foray into political and social counterinsurgency. Together, they demonstrated how covert warfare could tip the scales in an asymmetrical conflict—but also how such methods could spawn moral and strategic dilemmas lasting well beyond the final helicopter departure.

Key threads that define SOG's and Phoenix's collective heritage:

1. **Integration of Intelligence and Operations**: Modern special operations rely on swift, comprehensive intelligence—a standard largely shaped by the synergy between SOG's ground teams and Phoenix's infiltration of insurgent networks.

2. **Moral Ambiguities of Covert War**: While these programs could achieve swift tactical goals, the secrecy that shielded them also emboldened potential overreach, sowing controversy that endures today.

3. **Inspiration for Future Doctrines**: From SOCOM's formation to the "kill-capture" missions in recent conflicts, the blueprint laid by SOG and Phoenix informs ongoing practices—sometimes with

more refined oversight, sometimes repeating old mistakes.

4. **Resilience and Aftermath**: Veterans from both SOG and Phoenix grapple with unique burdens—victories overshadowed by secrecy, or moral trials unrecognized by the broader public. Their testimonies stand as a cautionary note for subsequent generations.

In many respects, the quiet heroism of SOG operators and Phoenix agents resonates through the decades, challenging us to parse covert success from potential ethical cost. Their experiences shaped not only the final chapters of the Vietnam War but also the continuing evolution of U.S. and allied special operations. As more documents surface and public discourse expands, the debate remains: did the clandestine path ultimately serve or undermine broader strategic aims? The answer, perhaps, lies in recognizing that the nature of secret warfare defies simple labels—like victory or defeat—and instead demands nuanced reflection on how best to wield power when so much hides in the shadows.

Conclusion

Remembering Their Sacrifice and Carrying Lessons Forward

When the conflict in Vietnam finally drew to a close, the names and deeds of MACV-SOG operatives remained hidden behind layers of classified information. Over time, details emerged that revealed both their daring exploits and the stark realities they faced. Today, we can reflect on how these men shaped not only the war they fought in but also the modern trajectory of special operations around the world. In this final chapter, we revisit the central themes of MACV-SOG's story—courage, secrecy, moral complexity—and consider how the lessons gleaned from their experience reverberated in subsequent U.S. conflicts, from Grenada and Haiti to Afghanistan and beyond.

Summarizing Key Insights

Covert Roles, Real Consequences

Throughout these chapters, it has become clear that SOG embodied more than just daring raids or clever tactics. Its activities took place within a broader tapestry of struggles: the moral ambiguities of waging war in Southeast Asia, the creeping doubts about foreign intervention, and the strain on both American and Vietnamese societies. Even as MACV-SOG missions operated outside official recognition, they left tangible impacts—on the flow of war matériel along the Ho Chi Minh Trail, on local populations uprooted by sabotage, and on the international understanding of American military reach.

For decades, SOG veterans carried a dual burden: The pride of having served in one of the most specialized units of the era, and the frustration of doing so in near-complete obscurity. Many also wrestled with the ethical implications of cross-border raids, sabotage programs, and engagements that blurred the line between combatants and non-combatants. Yet despite these challenges, their story remains a testament to the extraordinary resolve of small units taking on formidable foes under punishing conditions.

Empathy for All Sides Affected

War rarely conforms to clear moral boundaries, and the Vietnam conflict was especially tangled. Civilians became refugees, villages turned into battlefields, and neighboring countries were drawn into covert engagements. SOG operatives knew that their operations—whether inserting surveillance teams in Laos or sabotaging enemy convoys in Cambodia—might cause chaos for communities who had no choice in the matter.

This recognition sparks a deeper empathy: the veterans' accounts reveal not just adrenaline-fueled missions but also quiet, painful reflections on what it meant to disrupt people's lives, even while pursuing strategic objectives. Interviews in later years often highlight a hope that future conflicts might be handled with greater care for local populations, better communication with allied forces, and a clearer understanding of the end goals.

Lessons Learned: The Vietnam Loss and Future Conflicts

The U.S. did not achieve the objectives it set out for itself in Vietnam, and SOG's efforts, as remarkable as they were tactically, couldn't alter the wider political outcome. Still, the lessons gleaned from the conflict shaped the way special operations would be organized and employed for decades to come. Examining how these lessons were carried forward into later interventions—such as Grenada, Haiti, Afghanistan, and even

Task Force(TF) Black and TF Knight in Iraq—illuminates the enduring influence of SOG's methods and mindset.

Figure 18 – Delta force operators disguised as Afghan civilians

The Value of Integrated Intelligence

One key takeaway from SOG's experience was the power of blending human intelligence with real-time signals interception and aerial surveillance. The unit's successes (and failures) demonstrated that precise knowledge of the enemy's location, movements, and intentions could be decisive—even when numerical odds were stacked against small teams. This approach carried forward into missions in Grenada

(Operation Urgent Fury, 1983), where Special Forces collaborated closely with intelligence agencies to locate high-value targets and protect American citizens.[1]

Decades later, during the interventions in Haiti (1994) and early operations in Afghanistan (2001), the fusion of intelligence and special operations built on the Vietnam-era template. Veteran Colonel James R. "Jim" Davis, who served in Afghanistan, stated in a 2005 interview, "We took the lessons about flexible intel from MACV-SOG—how they could pivot quickly when new data came in—and applied it to our ground operations against Taliban hideouts."[2] The direct lineage of SOG's intelligence-driven ethos is evident in the modern U.S. Special Operations Command (SOCOM) structure.

Working by, With, and Through Local Allies

SOG learned early on that alliances with Indigenous scouts (like the Montagnards) or local paramilitaries could tip the scales in complex environments. This concept—partnering with local forces who understand the terrain, language, and cultural nuances—helped small teams move undetected and gather crucial insights. Similar strategies were employed during the 2004–2009 era of Task Force Black in Baghdad, an elite British-U.S. joint special operations group that worked with informants and local security forces to dismantle insurgent networks.[3]

Haiti, too, offered a clear example of the importance of local cooperation. While Operation Uphold Democracy (1994) involved a large conventional presence, small special operations detachments embedded with Haitian police and community leaders to stabilize regions and reduce violence. The capacity to build alliances on the ground owes much to SOG's early recognition that no technology or external force alone can substitute for local knowledge.

CHARLES J. MCARTHUR

Adaptability in Chaotic Conditions

A hallmark of SOG was the ability to improvise under extreme stress. Whether pinned down behind enemy lines or lacking sufficient air support, SOG teams quickly adapted their tactics. Future conflicts would demand similar agility. In Grenada, for instance, small special operations teams found themselves improvising landing zones and communications when conventional plans faltered.[4] In Afghanistan, rapidly shifting front lines meant that operators needed to pivot from reconnaissance to direct action within hours.

The concept of being "small but scalable" has become integral to modern special operations. Trained to handle everything from search-and-rescue to counterterrorism in unpredictable environments, operators today mirror the SOG mindset: prioritize stealth, coordination, and a willingness to adapt on the fly.

Restraint, Public Opinion, and Long-Term Strategy

The U.S. experience in Vietnam underscored that even tactically successful operations could lose broader support if they lacked clear objectives or overshadowed moral boundaries. SOG missions, conducted in secrecy, sometimes drew accusations of wrongdoing when fragments of information leaked. This tension between secrecy and accountability remains highly relevant. In present-day conflicts, such as Afghanistan and Iraq, special operations activities have faced intense public scrutiny. Collateral damage, treatment of detainees, and cross-border raids spark debates eerily reminiscent of those sparked by SOG's forays into Laos or Cambodia.

In TF Black/TF Knight operations in Iraq (circa 2004–2009), British and American special operators were hyper-aware of the political ramifications of each mission. They employed targeted strikes against insurgent leadership and Improvised Explosive Device (IED) teams, carefully balancing aggression with the need to avoid inflaming local hostility.[5] The legacy of Vietnam, in which a public backlash contributed to U.S. withdrawal, reminded commanders that public opinion can be as crucial as battlefield achievements.

A Final Tribute

Honoring Those Who Served in Silence

Many SOG veterans spent decades without public acknowledgment of their contributions or the dangers they faced. Over time, as partial declassifications and memoirs brought their stories to light, a wave of appreciation emerged. Former recon team member Michael "Mick" Hayes voiced relief in a 1998 open-source interview: "We were just doing our jobs, but we did feel forgotten for a while. Now, at least, people understand what SOG was and what it tried to accomplish."[6]

This shift in recognition led to memorials, unit reunions, and dedicated studies of SOG's missions. The bond among veterans remains strong; they stand as a living archive of experience that continues to inform younger soldiers, historians, and policy experts. A common refrain among these men is that their sacrifices, once locked behind classified files, hold lessons for avoiding mistakes and maximizing strategic gains in modern wars. Just like the British Ministry of Defence will never publicly acknowledge UK Special Forces' operations (SAS, SBS etc) US SOG operations remain hidden in secret files for decades. Their silent warriors' valiant endeavors are only ever known to a select few operators and their families. Highly classified missions are carried out globally, often with little known congressional oversight, furthering rumors of a 'black operations' force working beyond public scrutiny, often in locations the majority of politicians are blissfully unaware of, furthering some questionable political and military goal. This aside, the bravery, tenacity and loyalty of

the SOG operators can never be called into
question.

Reconciling Past Controversies

Every conflict inevitably weaves personal
suffering into its narrative. In the case of
SOG, the debate over cross-border missions,
sabotage, and secrecy still provokes polarized
opinions. Some veterans insist these missions
were indispensable for slowing the enemy's
momentum, while others wrestle with the
moral weight of clandestine acts that blurred
customary lines of engagement.

Yet many operators also speak of
gratitude—for having served in a tight-knit
community that looked out for one another,
for the moments of courage they witnessed
under fire, and for the chance to glean
insights that shaped future operations. The
sincerity of these reflections offers a nuanced
perspective: war is rarely clean, but profound
human connections can emerge within the
chaos.

Continuing Influence in the Modern Era

Today, small teams akin to SOG deploy in hotspots around the globe, from counterterrorism missions in the Sahel region of Africa, targeting and intelligence gathering roles in Gaza/Lebanon, to advisory roles in Eastern Europe/Ukraine. They carry advanced digital tools, but the essential nature of their work remains the same: step into uncertain zones, gather critical intelligence, and act decisively when needed. If anything, modern technology has heightened both the capabilities and the vulnerabilities of such teams, underscoring the timelessness of SOG's underlying lessons. SOG missions are designed to achieve strategic effects which is why in most cases their missions are kept secret and on a strict need-to-know basis.

Even as conflict takes new shapes—cyberattacks, drone warfare, and hybrid threats—there remains an understanding that small units, driven by grit, cultural sensitivity, and moral awareness, can accomplish feats that large conventional forces cannot. The Vietnam War may have receded into the past, yet the imprint of SOG on the American way of war remains both cautionary and inspirational.

A Human Endnote: Balancing Pride and Pain

As we close this exploration of MACV-SOG, it is crucial to remember the individuals behind every coded operation name and after-action report. Their experiences remind us that behind phrases like "covert warfare" and "clandestine missions" lie real people—families left to wonder about their loved one's fate, veterans carrying invisible wounds, and communities caught in the crossfire.

For many SOG veterans, recognition came too late to heal all scars. Still, their accounts and documented achievements illuminate a war that continues to shape U.S. foreign policy and military doctrine. The trials they endured underscore the complexity of sending young men into harm's way under classified directives. And the resilience they displayed offers an enduring testament to the potential for bravery, loyalty, and ingenuity even when grand strategies ultimately falter.

Closing Reflections

MACV-SOG's impact resonates across time, from the battle-scarred jungles of Vietnam to the digital battlefields of the twenty-first century. In telling their story, we gain more than an appreciation for clandestine heroism; we confront uncomfortable truths about secrecy, the human cost of unconventional warfare, and the lasting consequences of political decision-making in conflict zones.

Yet, amid these complexities, there is also hope. The men of SOG and their successors proved that skillful, disciplined, and empathic approaches to war can influence outcomes more profoundly than brute force alone. Their experiences beckon us to weigh the moral dilemmas they faced and to remember that the most profound challenge in war—then and now—lies in safeguarding humanity while contending with the relentless demands of strategy.

To any Veteran who picked up this book...

Thank you for your service

About the Author

Charles J. McArthur is a retired journalist, born and raised in West Virginia before venturing out on a life of travels. He spent much of his later career working and living in Asia, where he raised his own family. Having had a lifelong interest in military history, he now spends his retirement researching and writing on the subject so the true stories of courage and bravery may never be forgotten.

References

Introduction

1. Stanley Karnow, *Vietnam: A History* (New York: Viking, 1983), 14–17.

2. Bernard B. Fall, *Street Without Joy: The French Debacle in Indochina* (Harrisburg, PA: Stackpole Books, 1961), 26–30.

3. U.S. Department of State, "The Geneva Conference, 1954," *Office of the Historian*, accessed January 2025, https://history.state.gov/milestones/1953-1960/geneva.

4. Ronald H. Spector, *Advice and Support: The Early Years of the U.S. Army in Vietnam, 1941–1960* (Washington, DC:

U.S. Army Center of Military History, 1983), 80–83.

5. National Archives and Records Administration (NARA), "Vietnam War U.S. Military Fatal Casualty Statistics," accessed January 2025, https://www.archives.gov/research/military/vietnam-war.

6. Shelby L. Stanton, *Green Berets at War: U.S. Army Special Forces in Southeast Asia, 1956–1975* (Novato, CA: Presidio Press, 1985), 45–47.

7. William Rosenau, *Special Operations Forces and Elusive Enemy Ground Targets: Lessons from Vietnam and the Persian Gulf War* (Santa Monica, CA: RAND Corporation, 2001), 12–15.

8. John Singlaub, *Hazardous Duty: An American Soldier in the Twentieth Century* (New York: Summit Books, 1991), 131–36.

9. Richard H. Shultz Jr., *The Secret*

War Against Hanoi (New York: HarperCollins, 1999), 65–68.

10. Ibid., 85–87.

11. Alvin "Buck" Daniels, Interview by Southeast Asia Veterans Archive, 1985, University of California, Berkeley.

12. U.S. Department of Defense, *Declassified Records on MACV-SOG Operations*, partial release, 1990s, RG 472, Box 39, NARA.

13. James Elkins, Interview by Tim O'Donnell, 1992, *War Stories Archive*, Denver, CO.

14. U.S. Army Center of Military History, "Indochina—The War in Vietnam," accessed January 2025, https://history.army.mil/html/books helves/resmat/vietnam/indochina.ht ml.

15. Department of the Army, *Formation of MACV-SOG: Preliminary*

Directives, partial declassification, 1964, Special Operations Research Office, Washington, DC.

16. Rosenau, *Special Operations Forces*, 19–20.

17. Stanton, *Green Berets at War*, 120–23.

18. Karnow, *Vietnam: A History*, 274–79.

19. Shultz Jr., *The Secret War Against Hanoi*, 120–24.

20. Anonymous Specialist's Journal (1969–1970), Private Collection, archived at the Veterans History Project, Library of Congress.

21. James L. Nance, *Into the Laotian Jungle: Covert Reconnaissance in the Vietnam War* (Lexington, KY: University Press of Kentucky, 2003), 4–6.

22. U.S. National Archives, MACV-SOG *After-Action Reports*, partial declassification, various boxes,

accessed January 2025, https://www.archives.gov.

23. Harold Bishop, Interview by Dr. Nancy Bowers, Oral History Program (1990), University of Washington.

24. Nham Ju, Oral Testimony (translated), 1982, Southeast Asia Veterans Archive, University of California, Los Angeles.

25. John Prados, *Vietnam: The History of an Unwinnable War*, 1945–1975 (Lawrence, KS: University Press of Kansas, 2009), 291–94.

Chapter 1

1. Martin Thomas, *The French Empire Between the Wars: Imperialism, Politics, and Society* (Manchester: Manchester University Press, 2005), 112.

2. Bernard B. Fall, *Street Without Joy: The French Debacle in Indochina* (Harrisburg, PA: Stackpole Books,

1961), 259–61.

3. Pierre Bouchard, *Unpublished Diary*, January 1954, French National Archives (ANF), Paris.

4. U.S. Department of State, "The Geneva Conference (1954)," *Office of the Historian*, accessed January 25, 2025, https://history.state.gov/milestones/ 1953-1960/geneva.

5. National Archives and Records Administration, "Vietnam War U.S. Military Fatal Casualty Statistics," accessed January 25, 2025, https://www.archives.gov/research/ military/vietnam-war.

6. Nguyen Thi Lan, Letter to Nguyen Le Minh, May 1970, Private Family Collection, Austin, TX.

7. U.S. Department of State, *Foreign Relations of the United States*, 1958–1960, *Volume I*, accessed January 25, 2025,

https://history.state.gov/historicaldo
cuments/frus1958-60v01.

8. U.S. Department of State, *Foreign
Relations of the United States*,
1961–1963, *Volume I*, 237–40, accessed
January 25, 2025,
https://history.state.gov/historicaldo
cuments/frus1961-63v01.

9. U.S. Army Center of Military History,
"Indochina – The War in Vietnam,"
accessed January 25, 2025,
https://history.army.mil/html/books
helves/resmat/vietnam/indochina.ht
ml.

10. Robert Hills, *Personal Journal*, October
1959, Veterans History Project, Library
of Congress, Washington, DC.

11. U.S. Army Center of Military History,
Airmobility in Vietnam, 1965, partially
declassified, Carlisle Barracks, PA.

12. William Rosenau, *Special Operations
Forces and Elusive Enemy Ground*

Targets: Lessons from Vietnam and the Persian Gulf War (Santa Monica, CA: RAND Corporation, 2001), 18–19.

13. National Archives and Records Administration, "General Westmoreland's Private Memoranda on Covert Ops," RG 472, Box 39, accessed January 25, 2025.

14. John Singlaub, Interview by Military History Institute, 1978, Carlisle Barracks, PA.

15. U.S. Army, "Preliminary SOG Formation Documents," 1964, archived in the Special Operations Research Office, Washington, DC.

16. Paul Stevenson, Interview by Southeast Asia Veterans Archive, 1972, University of California, Los Angeles.

17. Tran Thi Huong, Oral History, 1990, University of Washington Southeast Asia Collection.

18. U.S. Department of Defense, *Vietnam War Declassified Briefings*: 1963–1967, partially declassified 1990, University of Houston Archives.

19. John Singlaub, *Private Journal Excerpts*, 1965–66, archived at the Special Operations Research Office, Washington, DC.

20. Thomas E. Heinl, *Ambush Tactics in Southeast Asia* (Washington, DC: Naval War College Press, 1974), 38–40.

Chapter 2

1. U.S. Department of Defense, *Records Pertaining to Covert Operations in Southeast Asia*, 1962–1964, partially declassified, GovInfo archives.

2. White House Memo, National Security Advisors to President Johnson, September 1964, *Declassified Presidential Papers*, University of Texas, Austin.

3. Pentagon-Saigon Correspondence, 1963–1964, RG 472, Box 14, National Archives and Records Administration (NARA).

4. Harold Bishop, Interview by Nancy Bowers, 1991, Veterans Oral History Project, Denver, CO.

5. William C. Westmoreland, A *Soldier Reports* (Garden City, NY: Doubleday, 1976), 128–30.

6. Shelby L. Stanton, *Green Berets at War: U.S. Army Special Forces in Southeast Asia 1956–1975* (Novato, CA: Presidio Press, 1985), 56–60.

7. William C. Westmoreland, A *Soldier Reports* (New York: Doubleday, 1976), 173–78

8. William Colby, *Lost Victory: A Firsthand Account of America's Sixteen-Year Involvement in Vietnam* (Chicago: Contemporary Books, 1989), 234–38.

9. John Singlaub, Interview by Military History Institute, 1978, Carlisle Barracks, PA.

10. Military Assistance Command, Vietnam, "Pre-SOG Field Directives," 1963, archived at the Special Operations Research Office, Washington, DC.

11. MACV-SOG, *Declassified Logs of Cross-Border Operations*, January–March 1964, RG 472, NARA.

12. Sam Robbins, Oral History, 1975, War Memories Collection, Houston, TX.

13. U.S. Department of Defense, "Operation Eldest Son: Psychological Operations Brief," partially declassified, 1970.

14. Tim Pollack, Interview by Tim O'Donnell, 1986, archived in Southeast Asia Veterans Archive, University of California, Los Angeles.

15. John Singlaub, *Private Memoirs* (Unpublished Manuscript, 1968–1970), Special Operations Research Office, Washington, DC.

16. U.S. Army Center of Military History, "Command & Control (C&C) Installations for SOG," partial release, 1988.

17. Robert Howard, "Motivational Address to SOG Recruits," 1972 transcript, Fort Bragg Archives, NC.

18. Martin Kim, Interview by Dr. Henry Sanders, 1985, Oral History Department, University of California, Berkeley.

19. Craig Wilton, Interview by Veterans History Project, 1979, Library of Congress, Washington, DC.

20. National Archives and Records Administration, "MACV-SOG Intelligence Summaries," RG 472, Boxes 45–47, accessed February 10, 2025.

21. Robert McNamara, "Confidential Briefing on Laos and Cambodia," 1965, partial declassification in 1992.

Chapter 3

1. U.S. Department of Defense, *Historical Office Internal Briefing: MACV-SOG Integration*, February 1965, National Archives, RG 472.

2. John Plaster, Interview by Military History Project, December 1978, personal transcript, Baltimore, MD.

3. James L. Nance, *Into the Laotian Jungle: Covert Reconnaissance in the Vietnam War* (Lexington, KY: University Press of Kentucky, 2003), 52–54.

4. John K. Singlaub, *Hazardous Duty: An American Soldier in the Twentieth Century* (New York: Summit Books, 1991), 197–99.

5. National Archives and Records Administration, "Declassified Records

of MACV-SOG Field Operations," RG 472, Box 42, accessed January 5, 2025.

6. Ronald Williams, Oral History, Veterans History Project, Library of Congress, 2004.

7. Christopher Robbins, *Air America* (New York: Avon Books, 1985), 112–14.

8. David Jensen, *Vietnam Helicopter Pilots Association Debrief*, 1972, Houston, TX.

9. U.S. Army Center of Military History, "Logistics Under Fire," accessed January 5, 2025, https://history.army.mil/html/books helves/resmat/vietnam/logistics.ht ml.

10. Anonymous Quartermaster, Interview by Tim O'Donnell, 1985, archived at the University of Texas at Austin.

11. Thomas Larson, Interview by Dr. Henry Sanders, Oral History

Department, 1975, University of California, Los Angeles.

12. Shelby L. Stanton, *Green Berets at War* (Novato, CA: Presidio Press, 1985), 86–87.

13. Daniel Becker, Oral History Recording, 1995, War Stories Archive, Denver, CO.

14. Sarah N. Croft, *Diplomatic Friction: State Department and Defense Department Tensions Over Covert Operations in Southeast Asia* (Boston: Beacon Press, 1992), 137–40.

15. Anonymous SOG Operative, Interview by Jane Thompson, 1974, archived at the Special Operations Research Office, Washington, DC.

16. Lydia Ortega, Memoir Excerpt, *Women in Vietnam Archive*, 1979, University of Houston.

Chapter 4

1. U.S. Army Center of Military History, "Cross-Border Operations: The Early Days," accessed January 10, 2025,https://history.army.mil/html/bookshelves/resmat/vietnam/cross-border.html

2. LRRP File #LRRP-1CAV-67-040 (declassified 2021), National Archives and Records Administration (NARA).

3. LRRP Summary, 101st Airborne Division (File #LRRP-101ABN-67-222), partial declassification, 2019.

4. Herman Cross, Interview by Tim O'Donnell, 1973, War Stories Archive, Denver, CO.

5. LRRP File #LRRP-25ID-69-027 (declassified 2021), NARA.

6. Tony Delgado, Interview by Dr. Nancy Bowers, Oral History Program, 1985, University of Washington.

7. https://www.vietnamwar50th.com/a ssets/1/28/Bargewell_Eldon_Captio ns_Transcript.pdf

8. U.S. Air Force Historical Research Agency, "Commando Vault: The High-Impact Bomb," Document 78-14, accessed January 10, 2025.

9. LRRP File #LRRP-173AB-68-155 (declassified 2020), NARA, referencing Dak To operations.

10. LRRP File #LRRP-4ID-67-119 (declassified 2021), NARA.

11. LRRP File #LRRP-25ID-68-144 (declassified 2020), NARA.

12. Allan Peters, Interview by Southeast Asia Veterans Archive, 1992, University of California, Berkeley.

13. LRRP After-Action Reports, 1967, partial encryption records referencing SOG ciphers, *Declassified Indochina Documents*, University of Houston.

14. 4th Infantry Division, LRRP Reconnaissance Logs, 1968, citing maritime contact.

15. LRRP File #LRRP-101ABN-69-302 (declassified 2022), discussing HALO sightings.

16. LRRP File #LRRP-1CAV-68-211 (declassified 2021), notes on rescue of a SOG operator.

17. Mike Randolph, Audio Recording, 1990, Public Archive, Memphis, TN.

18. https://www.vietnamwar50th.com/education/week_of_november_24_2024/

19. LRRP File #LRRP-173AB-68-098 (NARA) RG 472

Chapter 5

1. U.S. Army Center of Military History, "Equipment Modifications in Vietnam," accessed January 15,

2025,https://history.army.mil/html/ bookshelves/resmat/vietnam/equip ment.html.

2. National Archives and Records Administration, "Declassified Research on Foreign Firearms Used by U.S. Special Ops," RG 472, Box 77, accessed January 15, 2025.

3. Michael D. Locke, Interview by Southeast Asia Veterans Archive, 1972, University of Texas, Austin.

4. James L. Nance, *Into the Laotian Jungle: Covert Reconnaissance in the Vietnam War* (Lexington, KY: University Press of Kentucky, 2003), 65–67.

5. Will Ramirez, Oral History Recording, 1983, War Stories Archive, Denver, CO.

6. U.S. Army Special Warfare Museum, "Case Study: Knives of the Vietnam Conflict," 1986, Fort Bragg, NC.

7. U.S. Department of Defense, "Secure

Comms in Vietnam," *Classified Memo*, April 1966, declassified in 1990.

8. Fredrick Dawson, Interview by Tim O'Donnell, 1974, War Memories Project, Houston, TX.

9. Shelby L. Stanton, *Green Berets at War* (Novato, CA: Presidio Press, 1985), 113–15.

10. Sarah N. Croft, *Reconnaissance from Above: Air and UAV Innovations in Vietnam* (New York: Beacon Press, 1995), 49–52.

11. U.S. Military Assistance Command, Vietnam, "SOG Recon Team Composition and Duties," 1967 Field Manual (partially declassified 1995).

12. Joseph Kenyon, Memoir Transcript, 1970, Veterans History Project, Library of Congress.

13. Thomas E. Heinl, *Ambush Tactics in Southeast Asia* (Washington, DC: Naval

War College Press, 1974), 21–24.

14. David Jensen, *Vietnam Helicopter Pilots Association Debrief*, 1971, archived in Houston, TX.

15. Frank Holcombe, Interview by Dr. Henry Sanders, 1969, Oral History Department, University of California, Los Angeles.

16. Paul Jenkins, Interview by Nancy Bowers, 1979, University of Washington Oral History Collection.

17. Kyle Andersson, *Quiet Thunder: My Years with MACV-SOG* (Privately Published, 1981), 41–42.

18. William Rosenau, *Special Operations Forces and Elusive Enemy Ground Targets: Lessons from Vietnam and the Persian Gulf War* (Santa Monica, CA: RAND Corporation, 2001), 24–27.

Chapter 6

1. William C. Westmoreland, A *Soldier Reports* (Garden City, NY: Doubleday, 1976), 130–32.

2. John Singlaub, Interview by Dr. Raymond Brooks, 1978, Military History Institute, Carlisle Barracks, PA.

3. Jack Singlaub, *Dangerous Assignments: My Life as a Soldier* (New York: Simon & Schuster, 1988), 145–49.

4. Jack Singlaub, Private Letter to Colonel David M., August 1972, archived at the Special Operations Research Office, Washington, DC.

5. U.S. Department of Defense, "Coordination of Intelligence Assets in Southeast Asia," *Classified Briefing*, 1965, partially declassified in 1990.

6. U.S. Army Center of Military History, "Medal of Honor Recipients from MACV-SOG," accessed January 20, 2025,https://history.army.mil/moh/v ietnam-a-l.html.

7. Anonymous, Interview by Tim O'Donnell, 1973, War Stories Archive, Denver, CO.

8. Frank Greco, *Running Recon: A Photo Journey with SOG Special Ops Along the Ho Chi Minh Trail* (Philadelphia: Casemate, 2004), 58–60.

9. Ben Kline, Recollections of Recon, 1970, excerpt in Veterans History Project, Library of Congress, Washington, DC.

10. Shelby L. Stanton, *Green Berets at War* (Novato, CA: Presidio Press, 1985), 89–91.

11. Nham Ju, Interview by Southeast Asia Indigenous Heritage Group, 1981, Dallas, TX.

12. John Mason, Debrief Transcript, 1972, *Vietnam Helicopter Pilots Association Archives*, Houston, TX.

13. Anonymous Intelligence Analyst,

Letter to Colleague, 1969, Private Collection, West Virginia.

14. National Archives and Records Administration, "After-Action Reports and Award Citations," RG 472, Box 101, accessed January 20, 2025.

15. Gary Walker, Interview by Sarah Myers, Oral History Program, 1988, University of Washington.

16. David S. Lee, Interview by War Memories Project, 1990, archived in Houston, TX.

Chapter 7

1. U.S. Army Special Warfare Museum, "History of Border Surveillance and Special Forces Camps," 1971, Fort Bragg, NC.

2. Adam Reynolds, Interview by Tim O'Donnell, 1972, Veterans Oral History Project, Denver, CO.

3. National Archives and Records Administration, "After-Action Reports: Lang Vei Siege," RG 472, Box 90, accessed January 25, 2025.

4. Ray Delgado, Interview by Tim O'Donnell, 1975, Veterans Oral History Project, Denver, CO.

5. Shelby L. Stanton, *Green Berets at War* (Novato, CA: Presidio Press, 1985), 133–36.

6. Colonel John Singlaub, Internal Memorandum, February 1968, Special Operations Research Office, Washington, DC.

7. U.S. Army Center of Military History, "Dak To and the Central Highlands," accessed January 25, 2025,https://history.army.mil/html/bookshelves/resmat/vietnam/dakto.html.

8. Harold Fraser, Debrief Transcript, 1969, Special Operations Research

Office, Washington, DC.

9. James L. Nance, *Into the Laotian Jungle: Covert Reconnaissance in the Vietnam War* (Lexington, KY: University Press of Kentucky, 2003), 110–12.

10. Nick Townsend, Interview by Dr. Sarah Meyers, 1970, Oral History Department, University of Washington.

11. Luis Hernandez, Helicopter Door Gunner Debrief, 1969, Vietnam Helicopter Pilots Association Archives, Houston, TX.

12. U.S. Department of State, *Foreign Relations of the United States, 1964–1968, Volume VI*, accessed January 25, 2025,https://history.state.gov/historicaldocuments/frus1964-68v06.

13. Thomas E. Heinl, *Ambush Tactics in Southeast Asia* (Washington, DC: Naval War College Press, 1974), 38–40.

14. Robert Franks, Debrief, 1968, MACV-SOG Collections, Box 12, University of Houston.

15. Ibid.

16. Andrew Shelton, Letter to Family, May 1971, Private Collection, Orlando, FL.

17. Anonymous Field Artillery Officer, Interview by Nancy Bowers, 1971, Oral History Program, University of Washington.

18. Colonel John Singlaub, *Reflections on Covert Warfare* (Unpublished Manuscript, 1973), archived at the Special Operations Research Office, Washington, DC.

Chapter 8

1. CIA Archive #CIA-VN-67-103, *Declassified Vietnam Operations Documents*, accessed March 2025.

2. CIA Briefing, partially declassified

(1967), released 2020, University of Houston Archive.

3. https://www.vietnamwar50th.com/assets/1/28/Bargewell_Eldon_Captions_Transcript.pdf

4. CIA Cables referencing SOG-Eldest Son synergy, 1968–1969, *Declassified Indochina Documents*, National Archives and Records Administration (NARA).

5. MACV-SOG Field Report, RG 472, Box 58 (1968), partial declassification 2021, NARA.

6. Phoenix Program Cables, #PHX-67-112, *Declassified* 2019, U.S. Army Center of Military History.

7. https://medium.com/@therealistjug/operation-phoenix-the-cias-covert-counterinsurgency-program-in-vietnam-011f28cf58c3

8. Willis Beck, Interview (1974, partial

release 2022), *Veterans History Project*, Library of Congress.

9. CIA Station Memo, #CIA-PHX-69-045, 1969–70 period, archived at the Special Operations Research Office, Washington, DC.

10. MACV-SOG After-Action Reports, RG 472, Boxes 75–77, partially declassified 2021, NARA.

11. 1968 SOG Summary, *Interrogation of Political Commissar*, part of the MACV-SOG *Intelligence Summaries Collection*, NARA.

12. CIA Archive #CIA-VN-70-099, referencing Phoenix captures, partial release 2022, NARA.

13. CIA Training Manuals, *Urban and Rural Infiltration Tactics*, 1966–1971, partial release in 2021, University of Washington.

14. Raven (SOG Operator), CIA Debriefing,

1971, archived *Phoenix Program Collections*, University of California, Los Angeles.

15. Phoenix File #PHX-69-202, *Captured VC District Chiefs*, partial declassification 2020, NARA.

16. Harold Elkins, Interview by Dr. Sarah Meyers, 1988, *University of Washington Oral History Department*.

Chapter 9

1. U.S. Department of Defense, *Coordination of Covert Raids in Laos and Cambodia, Classified Briefing*, 1966, partially declassified in 1992.

2. David Porter, Interview by Dr. Nancy Bowers, 1995, Oral History Collection, University of Washington.

3. National Archives and Records Administration (NARA), "1967 Strategic Planning Memorandum," RG 472, Box 44, accessed February 2, 2025.

4. *The Washington Post*, "Leaked Documents Reveal Depth of Secret Raids," June 10, 1970.

5. Patrick Lin, Interview by Southeast Asia Veterans Archive, 1982, University of California, Los Angeles.

6. Lewis Gaunt, Oral History, 1990, War Memories Archive, Houston, TX.

7. Dominic Castelli, *Personal Journal Excerpt*, 1969, Private Collection, archived at the University of Texas, Austin.

8. Sarah N. Croft, *Diplomatic Friction: State Department and Defense Department Tensions Over Covert Operations in Southeast Asia* (Boston: Beacon Press, 1992), 177–80.

9. U.S. Army Inspector General's Report, 1974, partially declassified, University of Houston Archive.

10. John Gargus, *The Son Tay Raid*:

American POWs in Vietnam Were Not Forgotten (College Station, TX: Texas A&M University Press, 2007), 22–29.

11. William Martin, Audio Interview by Tim O'Donnell, 1971, Veterans History Project, Denver, CO.

12. Roger Leeds, Oral History, 1978, Military History Institute, Carlisle Barracks, PA.

13. Vietnamwar50th.com/assets/1/28/B argewell_Eldon_Captions_Transcrip t.pdf p16

14. Anonymous Interview, 1985, University of Washington Oral History Program.

15. Tina Morales, *Behind the Front Desk: Serving in MACV-SOG* (Privately Published, 1988), 51–53.

16. U.S. Congress, *Post-War Declassification Hearings*, 1984, GovInfo Archives, accessed February

2, 2025.

Chapter 10

1. U.S. Department of Defense, *Establishment of U.S. Special Operations Command*, 1987, GovInfo archives.

2. U.S. Army Field Manual 31-20, *Doctrine for Special Forces Operations*, 1978, partially declassified, University of Texas, Austin.

3. William Rosenau, *Special Operations Forces and Elusive Enemy Ground Targets: Lessons from Vietnam and the Persian Gulf War* (Santa Monica, CA: RAND Corporation, 2001), 24–27.

4. James Monroe, *Private Letters*, 1972–1974, partial collection archived at the Veterans History Project, Library of Congress.

5. Phoenix Program Cables, #PHX-70-213, *Declassified* 2018, U.S.

Army Center of Military History.

Conclusion

1. U.S. Department of Defense, *Operation Urgent Fury: Lessons Learned*, 1984, accessed February 7, 2025, https://www.defense.gov/.

2. Colonel James R. Davis, Interview by Dr. Nancy Bowers, 2005, University of Washington Oral History Collection.

3. Thomas E. Heinl, *Joint Operations in Modern Warfare* (London: J. Murray, 2014), 66–68.

4. U.S. Army War College, *Grenada: The Emergence of Special Operations as a Mainstay Tool*, 1985, Carlisle Barracks, PA.

5. Task Force Black Summary, British National Archives, declassified 2017, Kew, Richmond, London.

6. Michael Hayes, Interview by Southeast

Asia Veterans Archive, 1998, University of California, Los Angeles.

Picture Credits

Figure 1 –
https://commons.wikimedia.org/wiki/File:MACV-SOG.jpg

Figure 2 –
https://image.aladin.co.kr/Community/paper/2020/1025/pimg_7597791612711151.jpg

Figure 3 –
https://c2.staticflickr.com/8/7383/10501508656_1d5d0e2c03_b.jpg0

Figure 4 –
https://en.wikipedia.org/wiki/Donald_Blackburn#/media/File:Blackburn_visiting_MACV-SOG.jpg

Figure 5 –
https://en.wikipedia.org/wiki/20th_Special_Operations_Squadron#/media/File:USAF_UH-1Ps_over_Cambodia.jpg

Figure 6 –
https://vva.vietnam.ttu.edu/images.php?img
=/images/2499/24990605001.pdf

Figure 7 –
https://www.nationalmuseum.af.mil/Visit/
Museum-Exhibits/Fact-Sheets/Display/Arti
cle/3399200/prairie-fire-mission/

Figure 8 –
https://www.nationalmuseum.af.mil/Visit/
Museum-Exhibits/Fact-Sheets/Display/Arti
cle/3399200/prairie-fire-mission/

Figure 9 –
https://retrorifles.com/colt-xm177e1-gau-5-
car-15-1965-1966/

Figure 10 –
https://commons.wikimedia.org/wiki/File:R
ANDALL_MODEL_14_KNIFE_air_force.jpg

Figure 11 –
https://simple.wikipedia.org/wiki/John_K.
_Singlaub

Figure 12 –
https://www.cmohs.org/recipients/fred-w-zabitosky

Figure 13 –
https://www.cmohs.org/recipients/robert-l-howard

Figure 14 –
https://live.staticflickr.com/65535/51311278418_c4aab0c38f_b.jpg

Figure 15 –
https://commons.wikimedia.org/wiki/File:Phoenix_Program.jpg

Figure 16 –
https://en.wikipedia.org/wiki/Operation_Tailwind#/media/File:Special_Forces_Hatchet_Force_Tailwind.jpg

Figure 17 –
https://en.wikipedia.org/wiki/Fort_Liberty#/media/File:Special_Warfare_Memorial_Statue.jpg

Figure 18 –
https://en.wikipedia.org/wiki/List_of_oper

ations_conducted_by_Delta_Force#/medi
a/File:Delta_force_GIs_disguised_as_Afgh
an_civilians,_November_2001_C.jpg

Made in United States
Orlando, FL
26 January 2025

57795991R00157